# The Mediatorial Glories of The Son of God

seen in Tabernacle Patterns
and Sacrificial Types

James Green

Scripture Truth Publications

Original manuscript dated 10 March 1936

FIRST EDITION

FIRST PRINTING March 2021

ISBN: 978-0-9511515-6-3 (paperback)



Illustrated by the author
Photographs of the author's paintings by David Vernon

A publication of Scripture Truth



Scripture quotations marked (R.V.) are taken from "The Holy Bible containing the Old and New Testaments translated out of the original tongues : being the version set forth A.D. 1611 compared with the most ancient authorities and revised". Oxford: University Press, 1885.

Scripture quotations marked (J.N.D.) are taken from "The Holy Scriptures, a New Translation from the Original Languages" by J. N. Darby (G Morrish, 1890).

Cover photograph of a painting of the Tabernacle by James Green ©David Vernon

Published by Scripture Truth Publications
31-33 Glover Street, Crewe, Cheshire, CW1 3LD

*Scripture Truth is an imprint of Central Bible Hammond Trust, a charitable trust*

Typesetting by John Rice

The following pages
are dedicated by the Author
to the memory of
his Wife.

# Contents

# Illustrations

## Lists and tables

## Foreword

The author of this book, James Green, was a frequent contributor to early issues of *Scripture Truth* in the first part of the twentieth century. By profession he was an artist and lithographer, notable for his illustrations in Arthur Mee's *I See All* and subsequent *Children's Encyclopaedia.*

As he explains in the preface, his artistic talents were put to considerable use in a series of paintings produced to illuminate talks on the Tabernacle in the Old Testament. Appendix 2 reproduces an interesting leaflet inviting the receipient to attend a series of addresses by the author illustrated by these paintings. The paintings have survived in reasonable condition, and we are grateful to David Vernon, a professional photographer from New Zealand, who has photographed them for this, the first edition of a previously unpublished book, completed in 1936 towards the end of the author's life. A handwritten copy and a typescript of the original manuscript were made available, and the line drawings are taken from the latter.

For those who wonder why so much of the book of Exodus is taken up with a detailed description of an elaborate tent and its contents, this book provides an excellent explanation. For those who want to understand how such a description is evidence of the presence of "Christ in all the Scriptures", the author enthusiastically explores this theme in great detail.

He happily shares his appreciation of the glories of Christ obtained through detailed study of the Tabernacle. We are delighted to commend this book to you, with the prayer that in reading you too will come to appreciate in a life-transforming way what Jesus has done, is doing now, and will yet do for those who know Him.

*John Rice*

October 2020

**Note**: Editorial additions are enclosed in curly brackets thus: {addition}. Transliterations of Hebrew words conform to the conventions at the time of writing.

## Author's Preface

It was in the spring of 1917 that Mr Robertson of Bristol suggested to the writer the idea of making a series of pictures to illustrate the Tabernacle in the wilderness described in the book of Exodus. He felt that, while many models have been made, in using them for lecture purposes there is a considerable difficulty in a large audience seeing the details with sufficient distinction as the various vessels are of necessity small in proportion to the whole. He thought that large diagrams in colour would serve the purpose better. The scheme was carried out, the painting being commenced on June 2nd 1917 and finished April 4th 1918, having occupied 100 working days. The set of pictures were used on several occasions by Mr A J Pollock and the writer and were finally presented by Mr Robertson to Mr A J Pollock. In the summer of 1929 a new set was painted[1], this time on thin canvas so as to be easily carried by hand. The first set proved to be too heavy for easy transport, the boxes and contents weighing 110 lbs (50 kgs), whilst the latter

[1] The second set of pictures is in all respects similar in size to the former, with the exception of the general view which has been reduced to correspond in size with the other diagrams, 30" × 22". A ground plan and a chart of numbers has been added.

carried in a bag weighs only 11 lbs (5 kgs). The necessary study of the types has, under the hand of the God, resulted in a much fuller apprehension of the glories of Christ, conveyed in the patterns of things in the heavens, and at the request of his own family and brethren, the writer in the following pages, trusting to the grace of God and the illumination of the Holy Spirit, has endeavoured to set down the impressions he has received that others may profit thereby.

To God be the glory, and to our Lord Jesus Christ the praise for ever and ever.

# Part 1:
# The
# Background

# Chapter 1: Introduction

The book of Exodus has for its subject the history of a people brought from a condition of hopeless bondage under a tyrannical lord, into a place of nearness to God with His presence in their midst. The prominent thought, therefore, in the book is that of redemption, upon a basis which satisfies the moral character of God and meets the holy claims of His majesty. This was provided by the blood of the Passover lamb, so that God was able in consistency with the holiness of His nature to bring the children of Israel from under the yoke of the oppressor with a great deliverance, at the same time executing judgment upon their enemies. But further, they were brought out that God might bring them to Himself; hence He provided them with instructions for the making of a sanctuary, that He might dwell among them. On the line of His purpose their redemption was absolute and complete, at the same time God tested their reliance on this, and appreciation of His goodness, by proposing to them that their blessing should continue and depend upon their own conduct, that is, upon what they could be for Him. He gave them the Law at Sinai. Ignorant of the sinful state of their own hearts, the people accepted the conditions laid down, and the ways of God begin with them, in order that they might know themselves and finally trust in what God could be for them.

This is what every soul brought to God must learn, and what Israel will yet be instructed in, so that they shall no longer go about seeking to establish their own righteousness but shall submit themselves to the righteousness which is of God.

He who is the Lord our Righteousness is portrayed in the Tabernacle types of things in the heavens, but the vail is still upon the heart of Israel and they see it not.

May we with unveiled face behold therein the Glory of the Lord.

SCRIPTURES TO BE READ IN CONNECTION WITH EXODUS

Nehemiah 9:9-20
Joshua 24:2-7
Ezekiel 20:5-9
Psalm 105:23-43
Psalm 106:7-15
Psalm 136:10-15
Acts 7:17-41
Hebrews 7:1–10:39
Hebrews 11:23-29

### Divisions of the book of Exodus

The book of Exodus is readily divided into two parts. From chapter one through to the end of chapter fifteen verse 22 and then from there to the end.

| | | |
|---|---|---|
| 1. | Israel in Egypt | Chapters 1–15:22 |
| | Part 1 Bondage | Chapters 1–5 |
| | Part 2 Deliverance | Chapters 6–15:22 |
| 2. | Israel in the Wilderness | Chapters 15:23–40:38 |
| | Part 1 Red Sea to Sinai | Chapters 15:23–18:27 |
| | Part 2 The Law | Chapters 18:28–24:18 |
| | Part 3 The Tabernacle | Chapters 25:1–40:38 |

### The Tabernacle

The part of Exodus dealing with the Tabernacle can be divided into four sections.

| | | |
|---|---|---|
| Section 1 | Specification | Chapters 25:1–31:18 |
| | (a) The Tabernacle | Chapters 25–27 |
| | (b) The Priesthood | Chapters 28–29 |
| | (c) Worship | Chapter 30 |
| | (d) Workmen & Sabbath | Chapter 31 |
| Section 2[2] | Interlude | Chapters 32:1–34:35 |
| Section 3 | Construction | Chapters 35:1–39:43 |
| | (a) Workmen & Work | Chapters 35–38 |
| | (b) The Priesthood | Chapter 39 |
| Section 4 | Erection | Chapter 40:1-38 |

2 The interlude is concerned with the incident of the Golden Calf, and the second 40 days during which Moses is in the mount.

### Quotations from Exodus in the New Testament

| Chapter | Exodus | New Testament |
|---|---|---|
| Chapter | 3:6 | Matthew 22:32; Mark 12:26; Luke 20:37* |
| | 9:16 | Romans 9:17 |
| | 12:46 | John 19:36; compare Psalm 34:20 |
| | 13:2 | Luke 11:23 |
| | 16:18 | 2 Corinthians 8:15 |
| | 19:6 | 1 Peter 2:9* |
| | 20:12 | Ephesians 6:2-3; compare Deuteronomy 5:16 |
| | 20:12-16 | Matthew 19:18-19* |
| | 22:28 | Acts 23:5* |
| | 23:19 | Romans 9:15* |
| | 24:8 | Hebrews 9:20 |
| | 25:40 | Hebrews 8:5 |
| | 32:6 | 1 Corinthians 10:7* |

* Those marked thus agree with the Septuagint {LXX} version of the Hebrew text.

## The Figure of the True[3]

House mysterious, marvellous and holy,
All thy pattern given
By the hand of Him Who ere the ages
Built the endless Heaven.
As a mighty sign and wonder standing
In the vanished past—
Is thy secret unto us the aliens
Told at last?

Glorious House! foretold by sign and symbol,
Built by love Divine;
Shrine from whence the brightness of Thy glory
Shall for ever shine.
Set according to the pattern measured
Ere the world began,
For Thy dwelling to eternal ages,
Jesus, God and Man.

---

3 Adapted from Emma Frances Bevan, *The Last Parable of Ezekiel*, London: Chas J Thynne, 1900.

# Chapter 2: Preliminary Remarks

The glories of Christ as Mediator are presented in the Tabernacle patterns in the language of symbol and type, so that translated into the form of material objects which can be understood, heavenly realities may be described, which if told in the language of heaven could not be apprehended, for no words the human tongue can utter can set them forth apart from these figures. The typical presentation of the personal excellencies of the Son of God, Saviour, Sacrifice, Mediator and Priest is so interwoven into the warp and woof of Scripture, that perhaps we become unconscious of how much we are indebted to this method of making known the mind of God concerning His Son.

All Divine perfections pertaining to the Godhead were present in Him Who walked in lowly grace amongst men. He had emptied Himself of the outward form, but not of the essential attributes proper to Godhead, as Omnipotence, Omniscience, Upholder of all things by the word of His power; for these belong essentially to His Person as Son, and He could not cease to be what He ever was, God over all, blessed for ever. He did not use these attributes except as the Father should will, for He had taken a bondman's form and all was hidden behind the actuality of His Manhood, the veil of His flesh.

Before His incarnation every word He spoke was a command, but when the Word, the Divine Logos, became flesh, His whole life on earth was one of absolute obedience to the will of God, until He consummated this by the supreme act of obedience unto death, even the death of the cross. In all this the glory of God, of which He was the effulgence, was manifested in its full orbed moral splendour. In the Tabernacle types the shadow of this is given, yet not the very image; reflection indeed of coming glory, but not the substance; the pattern of things in the heavens, but not the heavenly things themselves. The ways of God in grace, entering into relationship with us feeble creatures, and the way by which approach to Him is provided are seen, nevertheless all is veiled, and that which is shown is a people with God, not as yet the supreme relationship of sons with the Father of our Lord Jesus Christ.

This was necessarily so, for the people were under the law which they had accepted, and in which they could find no liberty of access into the presence of God. It must be borne in mind that while the glory of the old covenant was a fading glory, which in due time would give place to the more excellent ministry of the new covenant, still, it was a perfectly righteous thing for God to propose terms of law, for had He not done so, the solemn question would never have been raised of man's competence to claim blessing from God on the ground of his own responsibility.

From the time that man fell, God had taken every care to show that His grace was the only hope for a fallen creature. But man was insensible to this, and therefore because his heart was filled with the conviction of his own self-sufficiency, the law of God put him to the test. The total inability of the people to stand before God on the ground of their own righteousness was soon made manifest in their breach of the first two commandments. This did not occasion any surprise to God, for before their sin He had said unto Moses, "Make thee an ark, and thou shalt put therein the law of the testimony which I shall give thee." It was the grace of God making provision for the accomplishment of His purpose, in order that no flesh should glory in His presence.

All that God had spoken, as applied in the letter of it, to man in the flesh could only condemn him for he did not answer to it, and the sacrifices ordained which could never take away sin were continually bringing sin to remembrance.

However blessed the ceremonial system was typically, it was literally a ministry of death and condemnation. All had an object, an 'end' on which we can now fix our eyes and see Christ. The 'end' was the glory of the Lord as the Mediator of the New Covenant. He has been into death for the redemption of the transgressions that were under the first covenant, has come out of it, and has gone up on high with the glory of all that God is in grace shining in His face.

Moses was not a quickening Spirit, nor could he give his spirit to the people, nor could the glory shining in his face bring them into conformity with himself. God's children now have the Spirit of the glorified Man in Whose face the glory of God shines. If we had not His

Spirit we should have no liberty to look on the glory of the Lord, or to see Him as the fulfilment of those marvellous types, which unfold the worth of His person and sacrifice.

The Temple is not presented as the pattern of heavenly things, it is connected with royalty and the establishment upon earth of the rule of the Son of David. For this reason in the epistle to the Hebrews, the Tabernacle only is mentioned. It is specifically a present thing, as Christ is in heaven now, and finally, when the holy city, New Jerusalem, descends out of heaven from God in the eternal state, the analogy is to the Tabernacle {Revelation 21:2-3}, whilst in the millennial condition the city is compared to the Temple.

The importance of the study of the Tabernacle lies in the fact that the fundamental principles concerning approach to God do not change, neither does the glory of Him by whose work has been secured this way of approach to the glory of God. Hence in these types, symbols, patterns and shadows of good things to come we have an outline of the truth displayed in pictorial form in such a way so that it may be easily assimilated in the light of the great message we heard of Him, "That God is light and in Him is no darkness at all."

## Chapter 3:
## Preceding Circumstances

Seven hundred and seventy-seven years had elapsed since the flood in 2348 B.C. when Moses was born and laid in the ark of bulrushes, 1571 B.C. After forty years in Egypt and forty in the land of Midian, he became the divinely chosen leader of the Exodus of the children of Israel from under the dominion and oppression of Pharaoh, King of Egypt, 1491 B.C. During the following year, 1490 B.C., the Tabernacle was constructed. The first three months of this year were occupied with the giving of the law on the 4th day, the two periods of 40 days, and 6 days connected with the incident of the Golden Calf: (4+80+6) equals 90 days (3 months). The construction of the Tabernacle occupied the remaining 9 months.

It is worthy of note that the Old Covenant contained in the ten commandments was established 50 days after the Passover, thus:–

The Passover was on the 14th day of the 1st month, leaving:

16 days in 1st month
30 days in 2nd month
4 days in 3rd month (Exodus 19:15;
50 days {compare 19:11, 16})

In like manner the New Covenant was ratified by the gift of the Spirit on the day of Pentecost, 50 days after Christ our Passover was sacrificed.

So terrified were the people by the sight of the devouring fire on Mount Sinai, that they begged Moses to draw near and hear the words that God would speak (Exodus 20:19; Deuteronomy 5:27). Moses drew near as the Mediator of the Old Covenant, and on the selfsame day, God promised to him that He would send a Prophet like to himself, a Mediator who should speak

There were 12 encampments under the cloud previous to the making of the Tabernacle (Numbers 33).

| | |
|---|---|
| 1. Rameses. | 15th day of 1st month |
| 2. Succoth. | |
| 3. Etham. | |
| 4. Pi-ha-hiroth. (Migdol) | Through the Red Sea. |
| 5. Marah. | |
| 6. Elim. | |
| 7. Red Sea shore. | |
| 8. Wilderness of Sin. | 15th day of 2nd month (Exodus 16:1) (manna provided) |
| 9. Dophkah. | |
| 10. Alush. | |
| 11. Rephidim. | |
| 12. Sinai. | 15th day of 3rd month of 1st year. (Leaving Sinai 20th day of 2nd month of 2nd year. {Numbers 10:11-12}) |

from heaven (Deuteronomy 18:15-19). This Mediator Prophet is depicted in the types of the Tabernacle.

In chapter 24, after sundry laws had been given and before Moses went up into the mount to receive from God the specification of the Tabernacle, there is presented an action symbolic of the Old and New Covenants. In the first case Moses with Aaron and his two sons Nadab and Abihu, with 70 of the elders are bidden to come and worship afar off. This is significant of all that the covenant of law, under which the people had bound themselves, could effect. Next follows the dedication of the first covenant with blood (Hebrews 9:18).

It has been suggested that the mention of young men, 'youths', offering the sacrifice indicates a new generation in contrast to the elders which stood with Moses (compare Psalm 45:16).

Until the question of sin was formally raised by the law, sin offerings have no specific place; the offerings in this case, as previously, were burnt and peace offerings, though the shedding of blood in these involved the question of man's condition, if not of actual transgression. Where no law is there is no transgression, nevertheless death reigned from Adam to Moses (Romans 5).

In chapter 24:3 the people repeat that which they had said before the law had been given, "All the words which the Lord hath said will we do" (Exodus 19:8). They say the same words again in verse 7. The importance of this is emphasised in Deuteronomy 26:17-18. It was their triple acceptance of the terms proposed. Whereupon the first thing Moses does is to write the law in a book, making it binding; then he sets up an altar with 12 pillars by it, identifying the whole of the tribes with the sacrifice of which the altar spake, in this case of judgment if the law was broken.

The witness of death was on the altar, the people and the book. On the altar, the penalty of death was seen; on the people, the covenant of the law was sealed; on the book, the conditions were unchangeable, it was the handwriting of ordinances, the breach of which brought condemnation.

Three times the blood was sprinkled, signifying death as the penal sanction of the law, the curse, the penalty of transgression. By the sprinkling of blood the people were sanctified, set apart unto obedience, with the sentence of death upon disobedience. Peter, in 1 Peter 1:2, uses similar language but with a great contrast caused by the addition of the name Jesus Christ, "Sanctified unto obedience and sprinkling of the blood of Jesus Christ." It is the blood of the New Covenant speaking of the completed, cleansing work by which sin is put away. In connection with this there are certain additions made by the Holy Spirit in His reference to Exodus 24 in Hebrews 9:19.

First, *water*, which speaks of moral cleansing; second, *scarlet wool*, which tells of consecration unto death for the cleansing of sin; third, *hyssop*, the lowest condition to which the mercy of God could descend for this object. These three are found in the Cross.

It was only half of the blood which was used in the above manner, the remaining half Moses put into basins, and nothing further is said about this in Exodus, but Hebrews 9:21-23 tells us moreover that the Tabernacle and all the vessels of the ministry were sprinkled, and that this was significant of purging and remission, pointing on to the much better sacrifice by which the heavenly things themselves should be purified.

In Exodus 40 we read of the Tabernacle being anointed with oil, but nothing is said about sprinkling with blood. The half of the blood in the basins appears to stand for this, and provides the reason for the following.

God ever had in mind the establishment of a new covenant which would be ratified not with the blood of bulls or of goats, but by the blood of the Prophet yet to come whom God would raise up. For this reason Moses and Aaron, representative of Christ as King and Priest, Nadab and Abihu indicating the priestly family, the 70 elders who stand for Israel, draw near, and five things are said concerning them:–

1. They saw the God of Israel.
2. They saw under His feet as the paved work of a sapphire stone.
3. They saw the body or form of heaven in clearness.
4. No judgment was laid upon them.
5. They ate and drank in the Divine Presence.

In these things there is a prophetic foreshadowing of that which was then far off, the good things to come of which the Tabernacle was a shadow:–

1. God, Who was hidden, would reveal Himself.
2. This would be by a work as intricate as a transparent mosaic of exceeding beauty, comparable to the deep blue of the sapphire symbolic of the manifestation of heavenly love. This would provide a standing suitable to the glory of God.

3. The absolute transparency of His holiness in heavenly splendour and purity would be manifest.
4. The accomplishment of this would eliminate judgment and provide a way of access to God.
5. The result would be the nearness of communion, the joy of home, the rest of God in His love, and the heading up in Christ of the heavenly and earthly families.

The Tabernacle may be regarded as the paved work of the sapphire. Its intricate detail, its surpassing beauty, its lavish wealth, set forth the wisdom, perfection and worth enshrined in the person and the work of the Lamb of God, Whose one sacrifice has opened the way for the display of the glorious reality of the heavenly things.

In Ezekiel 1:26 the sapphire is connected with the throne and the appearance of a man above upon it. In Ezekiel 10:11 it is associated with the cherubim. Speaking of the sapphire, F. W. Grant says:–

> "That of the ancients was, as Pliny testifies, 'refulgent with spots of gold — azure, never transparent.' When we hear God's voice claiming the heavens as His throne, how suited is the likeness of a sapphire stone! The word is derived from one (*saphar*) which means 'to number' and hence 'to tell' or 'declare'; and this is the word used when it is said that, "The heavens '*declare*' the glory of God" (Psalm 19:1). The sapphire throne, then, is symbolically just the starry vault, which is seen similarly on Mount Sinai, Exodus 24:10, when "they saw the God of Israel; and there was

> beneath His feet as transparent sapphire work, even as the heavens themselves for clearness". There is in what is seen, the general appearance of a sapphire stone, but with the added character of a transparency such as there is in the heavens themselves."[4]

For 40 days Moses was in the mount with God; the mention of Joshua in attendance would suggest the thought of conquest and victory — "Salvation of Jehovah" — which is significant in view of the Tabernacle instructions being given at the same time that the law was written on tables of stone, so soon to be broken. Joshua is significant of One Whom God had in reserve Who would accomplish all His purpose.

---

4 F. W. Grant. *The Numerical Bible: Being a Revised Translation of the Holy Scriptures with Expository Notes: Arranged, Divided, and Briefly Characterized According to the Principles of their Numerical Structure*, Volume 4: Ezekiel, page 22. Neptune, NJ: Loizeaux Brothers, 1931.

# Chapter 4: History

The history of the Tabernacle extends over a period of 600 years, that is from its construction in the wilderness until it was put by Solomon amongst the treasures of the Temple.

The writer of 1 Kings 6:1 does not say that the space between the two epochs was a period of 480 years. He records a fact which took place in the 480th year, and in doing so he only computes the years during which the children of Israel were under the direct government of Jehovah, and omits those years during which God sold them into the hands of the oppressors, a time equal to 114 years (see the book of Judges).

480 years of Divine government.
114 years of servitude.
__7 years Solomon building the Temple
601

The history of the Ark extends to the Captivity, another 430 years, and if, as is probable, the candlestick referred to in Daniel 5:5 is the original one, that would add another 70 years for this vessel.

The Tabernacle was carried by the children of Israel into Canaan, and after the subjugation of the land, it was set up at Shiloh (Joshua 18:1). At the door, Joshua and the heads of the tribes made the final division of the country (Joshua 19:51).

It was the presence of the Tabernacle in the midst of the land which made the possession of Canaan different from the portion of the 2½ tribes who had their inheritance on the east side of Jordan (Joshua 22:19).

We hear no more of the Tabernacle after the division of the land, (unless it was at Shechem when Joshua spoke his last words), until the circumstances surrounding the birth of Samuel, it being then at Shiloh, where it had remained during the days of the Judges (Judges 18:31). In the days of Eli a great change took place, when by the removal and loss of the Ark, "Ichabod", or "The glory is departed", was written upon the nation. To this the Psalmist refers in Psalm 78:60. From this time the Ark is never found again in the Tabernacle.

In the days of Saul the Tabernacle was pitched at Nob (1 Samuel 21). In the days of David the Ark was in Jerusalem, while the Tabernacle had been set up in Gibeon (1 Chronicles 16:39-40) and its order maintained (1 Chronicles 9:19, 27-32). It may have been moved from place to place as 1 Chronicles 17:5 seems to suggest, but its journeyings finally ceased by the order of David (1 Chronicles 23:26), and it remained in the high place at Gibeon where we find it at the opening of the reign of Solomon (1 Chronicles 21:29 & 16:39). The brazen altar made by Bezaleel was also at Gibeon, and Solomon with the congregation sought it, and upon it he offered a thousand burnt offerings (2 Chronicles

1:6). It was at Gibeon that God gave him the promise of wisdom and understanding (1 Kings 3:4).

The holy vessels with the Ark and the Tabernacle were put by Solomon in the Temple, 1004 B.C. (1 Kings 8:4 & 2 Chronicles 5:5). It was still found there in the reign of Joash (2 Chronicles 24:6), and remained until the captivity under Nebuchadnezzar (2 Chronicles 36:18). Whether any part of the Tabernacle was returned under the hand of Ezra we do not know, but there was no Ark in the second temple.

## The Pillar of Cloud

*The Pillar of the Cloud* had been the protection, guide and light of Israel from the hour of their leaving Egypt, and when the Tabernacle was completed, the glory of the Lord, known as *The Shekinah*, rested upon the Ark between the Cherubim. We hear no more of the Cloud after the crossing of the Jordan, but the glory seems to have remained until the days of Eli, returning when Solomon's Temple was complete.

Ezekiel in his first 10 chapters gives the description of its final departure, and prophesies of its return in a future day, when the name of Jerusalem shall be "Jehovah Shammah", the Lord is there.

Earth is dependent upon heaven at all times, and all fulness of blessing must come from above. In the Tabernacle is shown the pattern of the glory of Him, apart from Whom no joy can be. We may see also the shadow of a people who will fill the heavens with His praise. We shall see the forth-telling of a new world, which shall rejoice and blossom as the rose. Then shall He swallow up death in victory, wipe away tears from off all faces, and take away the reproach of His people from off all the earth: “For the Lord hath spoken it” (Isaiah 25:8).

## Chapter 5:
## God's Dwelling

Not built with hands is that fair radiant chamber
  Of God's untroubled rest—
Where Christ awaits to lay His weary-hearted
  In stillness on His breast.

Not only in a day of distant dawning,
  When past are desert years,
But now, amidst the turmoil and the battle,
  The mocking and the tears.

O Home of God, my Father's joy and gladness,
  O riven Veil whereby I enter in!
There can my soul forget the grave, the weeping,
  The weariness and sin.

Illumined with the everlasting glory,
  Still with the peace of God's eternal Now,
Thou, God, my Rest, my Refuge and my Tower—
  My Home art Thou.[5]

[5] T.S.M., translated by Emma Frances Bevan, *In His Tabernacle*, in *Hymns of Ter Steegen, Suso and Others (Second Series)*, London: James Nisbet & Co. Limited, 1899.

> ***"But will God indeed dwell on the earth? Behold the heaven and heaven of heavens cannot contain Thee; how much less this house that I have builded?" (1 Kings 8:27).***

Thus spake Solomon in wonder at the dedication of the Temple, but yet the desire to dwell with men originated with God. The principle thought in the Tabernacle is a dwelling place for God. "Let them make Me a sanctuary that I may dwell among them" (Exodus 25:8; Leviticus 26:11-12.)

The Hebrew word here in Exodus for sanctuary is *'miqdash'* — a holy place, and it especially designated the Holy of Holies, the place of the manifestation of the Divine Presence, suited to Himself, in order that He might dwell amongst the people. God desires the company of man, and it was for this purpose that He created him, that He might have a being with whom He could hold intercourse in mutual fellowship and joy. This great desire on God's part was marred by sin, for such a communion could only be in a condition which was suitable to God.

In the Fall, the response of affection was lost to God in the man He had formed, and the justice of God became a barrier to the outflowing of love to one who by an act of disobedience was amenable to His judgment. How this great thought of God, this desire to be known and enjoyed by man, has been made possible for a sinful creature is the wonder of the Gospel story.

The Tabernacle arrangements indicate the way of approach to God, and set forth in pattern the Person by Whom the way is opened, the work by which it is accomplished, and the result in the present time, and in a future day.

The Tabernacle is a type, a pictorial representation of spiritual realities. It is this because it expresses in form, colour and number an order of things which exist in the heavens and are connected with the great purposes of God. Moses was called up into the mount with God in order that he might be shown these great realities, and that which he was charged to make was to answer exactly to it. No deviation from or addition to the plan was admissible.[6] Thus he was admonished of God, "For see, saith He, that thou make all things according to the pattern showed to thee in the mount" (Hebrews 8:5).

The reason for making the Tabernacle is thus expressed, "Make me a sanctuary that I may dwell." On the part of the people there was to be willingness, for if God indeed is to have a dwelling amongst men, it must be with those who, constrained by His grace, willingly yield themselves to Him.

The Tabernacle was God's purpose, His plan worked out by man's work. The plan was Divine, the work was man's according to the pattern given. Two words are used: that in Exodus 25:9, 40, '*tabniyth*' translated 'pattern', literally 'model', suggests the architect's plan or model; nothing was left to human device or choice. The other word, used in Exodus 26:30, '*mishpat*' translated 'fashion' and rendered in Exodus 21:1 & 24:3 'judgments' and in Exodus 15:25 and Psalm 119:91 'ordinance', specifies rather the materials that are to be used.

In the joy that accompanied the deliverance at the Red Sea (Exodus 15:2), Moses and the children of Israel sang, "I will prepare Him a habitation" (A.V.), or "I will praise Him" (R.V.) or "I will glorify Him" (J.N.D.), the

6 How well this was carried out may be seen from the words "As the Lord commanded Moses" repeated fifteen times in chapters 39 & 40 at the completion of the work.

alternative translations not disagreeing in thought, for God can only dwell where He is glorified in His saints, and that by redemption. In Exodus 15:13 there is a distinct reference to the Tabernacle, "Thou hast guided them in Thy strength unto Thy holy habitation" (*'navah'* = home), and this present thing for them was to be the pledge of the fulfilment of all God's purposes for them as in verses 17-18, "Thou shalt bring them in, and plant them in the mountain of Thine inheritance, in a place, O Lord, which Thou hast made for Thee to dwell in, in the sanctuary (*'miqdash'*) which Thy hands have established. The Lord shall reign for ever and ever."

"Let them make Me": God was the Architect of His own house, and in this shadow of the house not made with hands, the construction was to be the product of the wise-hearted. Compare Hebrews 11:10 for the city of which God is artificer and constructor; Hebrews 9:11 for the greater and more perfect tabernacle; and 2 Corinthians 5:1 for the power of resurrection which then will be evidenced.

The materials for the earthly sanctuary were to be given by the willing-hearted (Exodus 25:2). Angels would have esteemed it a high honour if they had been permitted to provide this. It was to be a labour of love, not simply an act of creative power. Nothing is said as to God dwelling among His people until redemption had been, in figure, accomplished. On this ground, He had His sanctuary both in the wilderness and in the kingdom; now in the Christian dispensation, His redeemed are this, builded together for an habitation of God. In the Millennium, He will have a material sanctuary at Jerusalem; and finally, in the Eternal State, New Jerusalem shall be the tabernacle of God with men.

The Divine Presence is the greatest boon that can possibly be bestowed on the creature. It is the pledge of security, the secret of joy, the witness of the intimacy of love. The result is peace, and the effect is conformity to God's mind and will. In the realised presence of God, the heart and spirit revive, the practice of holiness is followed, the world is overcome, a true estimate of values is obtained and seen things give way to unseen. All this truly is the portion of each one who opens the door of his affections to the high and lofty One that inhabits eternity, whose name is holy, who, dwelling in the high and holy place, yet condescends to abide with him also that is of a meek and contrite spirit (Isaiah 57:15). Not only so, but the Divine Presence is the gathering centre for all who love His name. Wherever two or three are gathered to this, there in His presence may they realise the foretaste of the eternal joy. "In the midst of the assembly will I sing praise unto Thee." What then shall the sunshine of His presence be?

It was the great desire of David's heart to find out a place for the Lord, an habitation for the mighty God of Jacob (Psalm 132:5). How much more so should it be with us to whom the reality and not only the shadow belongs? God said to Moses, for his own personal rest and peace, "Certainly I will be with thee", but He also said, "Let them make Me a sanctuary that I may dwell among them." It was this that made Israel a distinct nation and when they lost this they were scattered to the four quarters of the earth (Exodus 33:14-16).

Fully displayed at last, the eternal blessedness of the Divine Presence shall fill Eternity, when in the midst of the throne and the living creatures and the elders, and the festal assembly of angelic hosts, shall the Lamb once slain be seen, Object supreme of all, by all adored.

His presence there, my soul
   Its rest, its joy untold
Shall find, when endless ages roll,
   And time shall ne'er grow old.

Our God the Centre is,
   His presence fills that land,
And countless myriads, owned as His,
   Round Him adoring stand.[7]

[7] John Nelson Darby (1800-1880)

# Chapter 6: Order of the Camp

We shall next consider how God set the people around His sanctuary, for this arrangement, like all else, was Divine in its ordering.

The Tabernacle consisted of a structure separated from its surroundings by a screen of fine linen, within which was the enclosure called the court, the whole being placed in relation to the cardinal points of the compass, and around this, as an inner guard, the sons of Levi had their encampment. Immediately opposite to the entrance, which was on the east side, were the tents of Moses and Aaron, with Aaron's sons who formed the priesthood. The rest of the tribe of Levi, that is the descendants of his three sons, Gershon, Kohath and Merari, occupied the remaining three sides. On the west side, behind the Tabernacle, were the families of the Gershonites, under whose care were the fabrics which composed the Tabernacle. On the north side, the families of Merari pitched, whose service was with the framework; while on the south side the Kohathites were placed, to whose charge the holy vessels were committed.

Correspondingly the twelve tribes (Manasseh taking the place originally filled by Levi), were divided into four divisions or camps, which were disposed with their standards thus:–

- On the east side the camp of Judah, consisting of Judah, Issachar and Zebulon;
- on the south side the camp of Reuben, having with him Simeon and Gad;
- on the west side the camp of Ephraim with Benjamin and Manasseh;
- lastly, on the north side the camp of Dan with Asher and Naptali;

the whole forming a double circle of armed guards to the sanctuary in the midst.

The same arrangement was adhered to on the march. The camp of Judah went first, followed by that of Reuben; then came the Tabernacle with its guard of Levites and priests, followed by the camp of Ephraim (compare Psalm 80:1-2), and the camp of Dan brought up the rear.

In practice the sons of Gershon and Merari marched between the camps of Judah and Reuben in order that they might arrive first to set up the Tabernacle in readiness to receive the holy vessels borne by the Kohathites.

On one occasion when Moses turned to Hobab his brother-in-law as to guidance regarding the place of encampment on the journey, this failure to recognise the wisdom and foresight of God resulted in the Ark leaving its central place and going three days ahead of the camp to search out a resting place.

The same thing has marked the pilgrimage of the Church of God. Human resources have been relied upon and the consequence has been the loss of Christ as Centre, though in grace He ever abides as Leader. He would have been none the less this for Israel and the Church if reliance had been placed on Him as the true centre of gathering, and He still is this for every true heart, as seen in the camp at rest.

Viewing the order of the camp symbolically, we may see that placed N.S.E.W. {at the four points of the compass} it has reference to outside influences which in a world such as this, the people of God must meet in the power of Him Who is among them. The journey is a warfare, the lodging place is a camp, and its order indicates the qualifications necessary to maintain steady progress.

- The camp of Judah has reference to *Righteousness*;
- the camp of Reuben to *Faith*;
- the camp of Ephraim to *Experience*; and
- the camp of Dan to *Exercise.*

The *camp of Judah* ('praise') was eastward, that is towards the sun-rising. This is the direction from which the east wind comes. So also the East speaks of the accomplished work and coming glory of Him Who has faced the east wind of Divine judgment, that the warriors of God might be armed with the breastplate of righteousness.

Judah's position contemplates the world as the place of malign influence and looks on to the uprising of the Sun of Righteousness which is to end such a state of things. He who faces in earnest the evil of the world will in proportion have as his outlook the appearing of Christ which will bring the disorder to an end. Romans 13:12 may well express the attitude which Judah's camp towards the sun-rising indicates: "The night is far spent, the day is at hand". Judah's captain is Nahshon ('the seer'). Judah is in the front rank because the spirit of praise is the evidence of power (compare 2 Chronicles 20:21-22). Judah is also the law-giver (Psalm 60:7), for the spirit of praise is followed by the obedient foot. In spiritual interpretation we may read on the standard of Judah, "Righteousness".

Actual standards were used for each of the four camps (Numbers 2:3, 10, 18, 25). Nothing is said as to their colour or design, but the Talmudists, basing their ideas on the blessing of Jacob (Genesis 49), give to Judah, a lion; to Reuben, a man; to Ephraim, an ox; and to Dan, an eagle. It will be observed in these emblems that there is a correspondence with the Cherubim (Ezekiel 1:10; Revelation 4:7).

On the South was the *camp of Reuben* ('see a son'). The South is the right hand (Ezekiel 47:1), the place of power and dignity, of peace, stability and blessing. The name of his captain is Elizur ('God is a rock'). The Reuben camp represents the security of everything established in the Son of God, and the overcoming faith which opens to the soul the world of God's purpose, compare 1 John 5:4-5. We may read on Reuben's standard, "Faith".

The *camp of Ephraim* ('fruitfulness') was westward, namely 'towards the sea' (Hebrew). From the West comes the refreshing wind loaded with moisture which produces fruitfulness. But the sea is also a type of trouble and unrest. To bring fruitful showers out of that which is a figure of sin, and its consequent trouble and unrest, is 'Grace'. The name of Ephraim's captain is Elishama ('God hath heard'), and we may read upon his standard, "Experience", for there is no fruit-bearing without this. At the same time the consciousness of Divine grace arms us against those who would deprive us of it (1 John 2:3, 3:14, 4:13). These things are not the foundation of peace upon which we build, Christ alone is that; but in the fight of faith we may yet find Ephraim to be the strength of the head (Psalm 60:7). The experimental knowledge of that which grace produces in the soul becomes like a helmet to resist the attacks of the sceptic, and to keep the mind from unrest and dizziness.

Lastly, the *camp of Dan* was on the North. The North has reference to what is hidden, and is connected with gloom and mystery. The most frequent attacks upon the land came from the north (compare Jeremiah 1:13-15 and Ezekiel 1:4). In the sides of the North the Babylonian makes his seat and defies the Almighty (Isaiah 14:13), but out of death comes victory, and upon the sides of the North is the city of the great King, the final victory after the exercise of conflict, when the Judge of all the earth shall assert His rights. So we may read on Dan's standard, "Exercise", and the name of his captain is Ahiezer ('brother of help'). Dan was the rearward of the host (Numbers 2:31), and it is just where our daily life touches the world that the attack of the enemy is felt most (compare Deuteronomy 25:17-18); and it is here that the judgment of God is most needed so that the senses are exercised to discern both good and evil. Here the sword of the soldier needs to be sharp if it is to separate between flesh and spirit, and to discern the thoughts and intents of the heart.

(Many of these suggestions as to the significance of the order of the camp are derived from the writings of F. W. Grant. See *Numerical Bible*[8]).

## The Camp of Levi

Not numbered amongst the tribes, they surrounded the Tabernacle on all sides. The sons of Kohath encamped on the South nearest to Reuben; the sons of Gershon were on the West side nearest to Ephraim; the sons of Merari pitched on the North nearest to Dan; whilst the

8 F. W. Grant. *The Numerical Bible: Being a Revised Translation of the Holy Scriptures with Expository Notes: Arranged, Divided, and Briefly Characterized According to the Principles of their Numerical Structure.* Neptune, NJ: Loizeaux Brothers, 1931.

priests, the sons of Aaron, encamped on the East, in proximity to Judah.

Whilst the four camps of Israel were a guard from the influences that might come from the outside, the Levites kept the people from the wrath that would follow intrusion into holy things. These holy vessels with the Tabernacle structure and fabrics were typical of the person of Christ, and all concerning this needs to be guarded with holy reverence and anything that detracts from His glory to be shunned. A Levitical character of ministry which attracts the heart to the glories of Christ is the best antidote to the reasonings of the human mind which would intrude into that which belongs only to God (Matthew 11:27), and which He only can comprehend.

*Kohath* – 'assembly' – was the second son of Levi; of his family the sons of Aaron were called to the priesthood; the remainder of his sons had committed to their care all the holy vessels, ark, table, lampstand, altars, etc. with the veil, which latter set forth the holy humility of Christ. The service of the Kohathites was symbolic of the truth which reaches as high as Christ in glory; it was therefore objective and connected with faith. Kohath may represent for us *the anointed ear*.

*Gershon* – 'exile' or 'stranger' – was the eldest son of Levi, and his sons had charge of all the fabrics, those things which, in the Tabernacle, speak of practical righteousness. Typically they were occupied with that which is subjective and to this belongs love. All this was exhibited in the pathway of our Lord. The Gershonite may therefore illustrate *the anointed foot*. From the spirit of strangership springs the purity of walk and freedom from the defilements of the world, at the same time the report of things not seen provides an object for the heart. In every office which our Lord fills, He exhibits the response of love in man to Divine love.

*Merari* – 'bitter' – was Levi's third son. To him and his sons the burden of the heavy structural parts, boards, bars, pillars, etc. was committed, hence their service had the character of labour and work. Merarite service may be symbolic of the labour involved in the support, strengthening, and steadying of the witness of God in this world. Merari will illustrate *the anointed hand*. The path and sufferings of our Lord on earth, the contradiction which He endured of sinners against Himself, is the pattern of the way all service for His name must take, and such service is necessarily accompanied by sorrow and bitterness, indeed as 2 Corinthians 2:4 shows, it is often so in relation to the assemblies of God.

The three characters of Levitical service may be seen in Ephesians 4:12:–

- The perfecting of the saints: Kohath
- The work of the ministry: Geshon
- The edifying of the body of Christ: Merari.

The priests, the sons of Aaron, had their service in connection with the holy vessels, the sacrifices and the incense, all of which were descriptive of worship as far as this extended under the economy of law, which worship stands in contrast to the nearness which it is the privilege of God's children now to know, and to the Spirit which draws near into the Holiest of all, to adore the God and Father of our Lord Jesus Christ.

The Christian is also called to walk in relation to the camp as one of the common people, filling the daily round, and in this exhibiting the practice of the truth which is its surest defence. Then as a Levite, he has, as may be assigned by God, his service in connection with the ministry of the Word, and in relation to the saints of God. This may take various forms, some hidden, some more prominent, but all under the control of the Spirit of worship, characteristic of the holy and royal priesthood to which all believers belong in the house of God over which our Lord Jesus Christ is great High Priest.

## Chapter 7: Names of the Tabernacle

The two principle ones are those which speak of it as *a meeting place.*

- '*ohel-mo'ed*' as in Numbers 18:6 (*mo'ed* = 'appointed place')

  The Tabernacle of the congregation or tent of meeting, where God could be approached by, and hold converse with, men. There they met God and one another.

- '*ohel-eduth*' as in Numbers 17:8.

  The Tabernacle of witness or tent of testimony, for its presence was the token of God's revelation and truth, where this was maintained and any further communications made. ('*eduth*' is also used of the law, God's declaration of His will.)

Then there are names which refer to the Tabernacle as *a dwelling place.*

- The tabernacle ('*mishkan*') of the Lord, Numbers 17:13.
- The house ('*bayith*') of the Lord, Joshua 6:24.

- The house ('*bayith*') of God, Judges 18:31.
- Thy holy habitation ('*maon*' = 'an abode'), Exodus 15:2; 1 Samuel 2:29.
- The temple ('*heykal*' = 'a palace') {of the Lord}, 1 Samuel 1:9 & 3:3.

  '*heykal*' is translated 'palace' (Psalm 45:8; Proverbs 30:28).

As a meeting place, the Tabernacle was the centre of the camp of Israel for their blessing and protection; as a dwelling place, it was for the exhibition of the glory of God, and that He might have an abode in their midst.

Then there are two names which designate the Tabernacle as *a holy place*:

- A sanctuary ('*miqdash*') Exodus 25:8.
- The sanctuary ('*kodesh*') Exodus 36:1.

The latter word is the root from which the former is derived.

'*Kodesh*' refers to the ceremonial act of cleansing, '*miqdash*' to the place that is so cleansed. The prefix '*m*' indicates this, meaning 'whatever' or 'that which'. The thought underlying '*kodesh*' is to separate or set apart, in the case of the Tabernacle to bring into contact with God for His special use. We use the word 'holy' so frequently to represent moral or spiritual qualities, that we lose the idea of holiness as relating to some position or existing relationship between God and the place, person or thing in question. Jeremiah is thus spoken of as sanctified ('*kodesh*') to God before he was born (Jeremiah 1:5), which does not mean that he was cleansed from original sin or regenerated by the Holy Spirit, but that he was thus separated early in God's purpose to the work in which he was to be used.

There are two other words employed in connection with the Tabernacle as *the gathering place* for the assembly or congregation:

- *'hedah'* meaning the corporate unity or assembly (Numbers 10:2-3), and
- *'kahal'* meaning the actual gathering (Deuteronomy 18:16), much as we might speak of an assemblage of people.

Israel was rejected on a twofold ground; first, they failed to bear witness to the unity of the Godhead as against idolatry, and their judgment for this was the captivity under Assyria and Babylon. Secondly, they rejected Jehovah in the person of His Son and their present state is the consequence.

From their first condition of judgment Cyrus was their partial deliverer; from the second Christ will be their Deliverer completely. But in the midst of all this God has a remnant which in the first case was brought back from Babylon (see Ezra & Nehemiah); in the second case, before the nation is restored, a remnant will be associated with the risen Christ on redemption ground, and in their midst He will sing praise (Psalm 22:22; Hebrews 2.12). They will thus be gathered into a *'kahal'*, an actual gathering founded on His atoning sacrifice and the power of life belonging to His resurrection, and with them the Divine Presence will be identified.

The 120 disciples in Acts 1 may illustrate this. But Israel will not be a corporate unity, an *'hedah'*, until the visible manifestation of Christ shall gather together His elect from the four winds, and the nation shall become one (see Ezekiel 37:16-22). But something has taken place before this, namely the baptism of the Spirit (Acts 2), which formed the Church, the Assembly, and to this the remnant of Israel is now added (Acts 2:47), losing their national standing and being incorporated, with the Gentiles who believe, in the Body of Christ. In the latter tribulation days the spared remnant will become the nucleus of the body of Israel (Psalm 72:16). Before the Spirit came, the 120 in the upper room were in actual gathering – '*kahal*' – but by the baptism of the Spirit they became a corporate body – '*hedah*' – and being thus owned by the Lord as His assembly they were a true '*ohel-moed*' ('tent of meeting'), for He was there.

This must not be confused with the organic unity of the Church in Ephesians, which is there seen united to a Head in heaven; the words spoken of above refer to that which is at present seen on earth.

## Chapter 8:
## The Materials

We are now prepared to consider the materials of which the Tabernacle, by Divine direction, was constructed. All of these considered separately are symbolic of spiritual realities. They fall into five groups:–

1. METALS *gold, silver, copper.*
   These represent Divine attributes.

2. FABRICS *blue, purple, scarlet, byssus, goats' hair, red rams' skins, badger skins.*
   These belong to Divine manifestation.

3. TIMBER *acacia wood.*
   This concerns the Person in Whom the manifestation is made.

4. OIL *olive oil.*
   A figure of the Holy Spirit.

5. SPICES & JEWELS *spices, with onyx & other precious stones.*
   These speak of the results produced by the Spirit.

It will be observed that the Triune God, Father, Son and Holy Spirit are symbolised by these materials. They were provided by the people whose hearts were made willing. God loveth a cheerful giver, and whether for the Tabernacle (Exodus 25), the Temple (1 Chronicles 29:1-9), or for the second temple (Ezra 2:68), it was a freewill offering that was provided (compare 2 Corinthians 8:10-15; 2 Corinthians 9:7; 1 Corinthians 16:1). The required offering flowed out in abundance from willing hearts, made willing by the grace of God, until there was so much that the people had to be restrained from bringing more (Exodus 36:4-6).

They thus enjoyed the privilege of contributing materials from which Jehovah's dwelling place was formed, and each of which was emblematic of some ray of His glory. The men gave that which set forth the Lord Jesus Christ in His various characters. The industry of the women spun the fabrics which showed forth His personal perfections. The rulers gave the things of value connected with position and worship.

## Metals

### Gold

In regard to the metals, gold takes the first place, as it is the first metal mentioned in Scripture (Genesis 2:11-12). It was used solid and also as a covering upon the wood of the Tabernacle. In the first case the solid pure gold is a symbol of the glory of God, His attributes of righteousness, holiness, wisdom, power, goodness and truth. It is an emblem of the Divine prerogatives. When used upon the wood it represents Deity in connection with humanity, the Divine glory of the Son of God. It was used in a third way, drawn out into wires and thus wrought into the fabrics, as in the case of the ephod worn by the High Priest. In this case it would set forth the Divine and acceptable righteousness in which Christ exercises His priesthood.

The thought of Deity is so closely connected with gold that it was frequently employed for idolatrous uses. For instance the Golden Calf (Exodus 32:1-4), the two calves that Jeroboam made (1 Kings 12:26-33) and the image made by Nebuchadnezzar (Daniel 3:1). Its true symbolism is clearly expressed in the Holy City (Revelation 21:18-21) as the righteousness of God, to which is added the thought of transparency and clearness, for in the City God is seen fully revealed in light, which the patterns of things in the heavens could not set forth. Gold is also marked out by its durability, it lasts indefinitely under the severest tests. It thus admirably describes God as the only eternal and unchanging One in all His attributes. Again, gold is the most ductile of all metals, a grain of it can be beaten out to cover 56 square inches or drawn into a wire 500 feet long. Thus it most beautifully speaks of the far-reaching grace and mercy of God (Exodus 34:5-7), and of the riches of His wisdom and knowledge (Romans 11:33).

### Silver

With the exception of the overlaying of the chapiters of the pillars of the court, silver was always used solid. This exception would seem to point to the purpose for which the Word became flesh, namely Redemption, and this being accomplished, it is seen as the foundation upon which the House of God stands. As a symbol it stands for God's grace shown in Christ Jesus in redemption.

The silver used in the Tabernacle was provided by the atonement money which each had to pay (Exodus 30:11-16). The occasion when this was given was

"When thou numberest the people". In this numbering each man was brought individually before God and each was reminded of their condition and consequent need of redemption. The rich and poor were all to give alike, for in this there was no difference, each needed a ransom for their souls. Then the object was "that there be no plague". If a sinner is brought under the eye of God, judgment must follow, unless at the same time he is under the protection of atonement. We have an instance of numbering the people and neglecting to take the ransom {atonement} money in the case of David (2 Samuel 24) and the plague that consequently followed. The silver of the ransom money speaks of the value of the blood of Christ (1 Peter 1:18-19). It will be observed that Peter speaks of gold as well as silver, for on one special occasion after a striking deliverance, gold was offered to God instead of silver (Numbers 31:49-54).

The sum prescribed was half a shekel (Exodus 38:25-26). A shekel is 20 *gerahs*, so that 10 *gerahs* was the amount given, and as 10 is the number of responsibility of man to God, it was the acknowledgment that this must be met in God's appointed way.

### Copper

— not brass as in the Authorized Version. The pure metal was used, not an alloy such as brass, of copper and zinc. It symbolizes the righteousness of God when sin is in question; it differs from the meaning of gold, which is also the righteousness of God but according to His nature, that which He always must be, and ever was, even before sin began to be.

Copper is the metal which can endure fire, and is a great conductor of heat. It was therefore most suitable for the vessels which typified the Lord enduring the fire of the judgment of God against sin. It was used in the solid form and also for overlaying. In the latter is seen the action of sacrifice, and in the former, its accomplishment.

### Quantity of Metal

{The modern equivalent weight of a talent is not certain. The author uses estimates based on the typical weight of marked ancient artifacts.} The *weight of metal* employed (see Exodus 38:21-31) was as follows:–

- Of gold, 29 talents and 730 shekels; reckoning a talent to weigh 131 lbs, the total would be 1½ tons.
- Of silver, 100 talents and 1,775 shekels; which taking a talent to weigh 117 lbs, the total would be 5 tons.

The silver was obtained from the atonement money. Each man above 20 years old gave a *bekah* (½ shekel). There were 603,550 men, therefore the amount of silver subscribed was 301,775 shekels. 1,775 shekels were used for hooks, rods and capitals; 300,000 shekels were used for the making of the 100 sockets which formed the foundation of the house. Each socket weighed 1 talent or 117 lbs. A talent equals 3,000 shekels, therefore each socket represented the ransom money of 6,000 men.

- Of copper, 70 talents, 2,400 shekels; which reckoning 135 lbs per talent, would equal 4 tons.

The number of people in the camp of Israel was 2½ million, and the value of the materials employed has been estimated at £250,000 {1936 value}.

## Fabrics

The symbolism of the *fabrics*, blue, purple, etc. will be best considered in the use to which they were put in making the hangings of the Tabernacle.

## Timber

### Acacia Wood

— the shittim wood of the Authorized Version. The '*shittah*' was a timber tree of considerable size, and the only tree available in the desert of Sinai. Its wood is incorruptible, extremely light and excels in strength, capability of polish and beauty. The fragrance of its blossoms entitle it to be named alongside the myrtle. The Septuagint calls it *xylon asepton* (*ξύλων ἀσήπτων*) — incorruptible wood. Altogether it is a very apt symbol of the holy humanity of our Lord Jesus Christ, seen in Him Who in sinless nature was not amenable to death, and Who having entered into death, the tree cut down, saw no corruption — the perfect Man Whose moral graces ever yielded sweet perfume in the midst of a desert world (compare Isaiah 41:19). The acacia is known today as the source of the gum arabic of commerce.

## Oil

— for the light and anointing. The only source of light in the Divine economy is the Holy Spirit, and He only can produce the fragrance sent forth by the spices.

## Spices and Jewels

{*Spices* are considered later, in the context of the Holy Anointing Oil (page 171) and the Incense (page 179).}

### Precious Stones

Each of these is for the display of some special glory of Christ and the manifestation of His excellence and perfection.

*Colour* is prominent in the Tabernacle; in Solomon's temple it is found only in the vail (2 Chronicles 3:14) and in that of Ezekiel there is none.

## The Workmen

In Exodus 31 there are three parts: verses 1-6, the workmen; verses 7-11, the work to be made; verses 12-18, the object to be attained — the Sabbath of rest.

The workmen were the gift of God, all the wisdom and understanding that they needed proceeded from God through the action of the Holy Spirit. God also endowed them with the capacity to teach others. In these workmen a pattern is provided of all true servants in every dispensation.

Human skill, wisdom or invention would have marred the Divine design, therefore in their filling of the Spirit of God, no room was left for this. The will of God was to be done, the mind of God carried out — "All that I have commanded thee" (verses 6 & 11). The work they were to make was not to be for their own glory.

> "The whole work of the Tabernacle in its exquisite perfection, and in its glorious beauty was the outshining of the work of the Holy Spirit. No man was glorified in that upreared Tabernacle. Men who with spiritual minds looked upon it would not say, 'How cunning a workman was Bezaleel', but rather 'See how wondrously the Spirit of God has wrought

> through Bezaleel in the accomplishment of the Divine purpose.'"[9]

The first workman in order was Bezaleel, who may represent for us a servant occupied with the objective side of truth. His name means 'shadow or protection of God'. He was the son of Uri ('light'), who was the son of Hur ('white or purity'), and he belonged to the tribe of Judah ('praise').

The second was Aholiab, whose name means 'tent or abode of his father'. He presents perhaps the subjective side of truth. He was the son of Ahisamach ('brother of support or help'), and his tribe was that of Dan ('judge or discerner').

Then was added the large number of workers each of whom had assigned to them their part in the service of the whole. No man could presume to appoint himself or another to the work of the Tabernacle, and although some of these workers may have only been appointed to do such humble work as fetching and carrying, yet all served the interests of the Sanctuary.

The Tabernacle was a shadow of good things to come; therefore in verses 12-17 the Sabbath is brought in, the rest of God to which all service leads (Hebrews 4:9-10), verse 18 indicating the culmination of the millennial seventh day of rest, in the eternal witness to the will of God (compare 1 Corinthians 15:28).

---

9 {Dr G. Campbell Morgan, *The Spirit of God*, Hodder and Stoughton, 1900.}

# Chapter 9: Symbols

Apart from the language of symbol, God could not communicate His thoughts to men, for human language adapted to earthly things is inadequate to convey in direct expression the spiritual conceptions with which the mind of God is occupied. The whole created realm is symbolic of that which exists in the heavens. It has been created not only by God, but for Him and in Him (Colossians 1:16), that is, bearing the impress of His character and the exhibition of His glory (Psalm 19:1; Revelation 4:11). Therefore the spiritual laws which are supernatural, are reflected in the things that are made. It is this fact which makes symbolism and parable possible, and reveals the eternal power and divinity of God as the secret of the universe (Romans 1:20). "For of Him and through Him and for Him are all things: to Him be glory for ever, Amen" (Romans 11:36, J.N.D.).

A *symbol* is an object, animate or inanimate, standing for, representing or calling to mind something moral or intellectual, an emblem. Salt, for instance, is a symbol of friendship; the symbol of addition is +; a flag is a symbol of a country or nation; a wedding ring is a symbol of marriage; a triangle is a symbol of the triune God. It will be evident from this that to interpret symbols literally is unsuitable and false in principle, and in many cases the attempt to depict symbols by pictures produces an absurdity, as for instance, a beast with seven heads and ten horns. The language of symbol is as definite as other forms of speech, and is always used in the same sense and meaning. Leaven is a symbol of the working principle of evil, never of good. Symbols present to the mind, in a concrete form and image, certain abstract qualities and facts, giving the moral characteristics which, in God's eyes, designate the thing spoken of. If we seize the moral bearing of symbols, we have a large introduction into the mind and purpose of God, and see things with His vision.

A symbol is more than a figure or illustration whose use is to make more vivid that which is mentally known, for by the elements or objects which it borrows, it creates a new idea, expresses a new fact, and there is frequently in it a combination of elements, whilst the type is more simple. But whether symbol or type, the spiritual facts conveyed by earthly means belong to one another by an inward necessity. As Archbishop Trench remarks,

> "It is not a happy accident which has yielded so wondrous an analogy as that of husband and wife to set forth the mystery of Christ's relation to His elect Church (Ephesians 5:23-32). There is far more in it than this: the earthly relation is indeed but a lower form of the heavenly on which it rests, and of which it is the utterance."[10]

10 Richard Chenevix Trench, *Notes on the Parables of Our Lord*, London: John W. Parker and Son, 1853, pages 11-12.

Truly heaven is not a dream of earth, but earth is the shadow of heaven.

The symbolic facts and objects which Scripture affords enter into the whole conception and framework of our religious thought, and one who possesses the truth through the medium of the symbol, will have a far stronger hold upon it, will be influenced by it far more mightily, and be more really nourished by it, than he possibly could be without it. At the same time there is a natural delight in this manner of communicating the truth, for it appeals to the imagination and feelings, and unconsciously fixes itself upon the memory. Such symbols as the bread and wine in the Lord's Supper, the water of baptism, and our Lord's allusion to Himself as "The Door", "The Shepherd", "The Vine" are cases in point.

The whole Levitical constitution with the Tabernacle arrangements, sacrifices and ordinances is declared in Hebrews 9:9 to be the symbol of higher things in the heavens.

The *type* differs somewhat from the foregoing, for it is the original reality in the mind of God, as Christ was God's typical man. The things which represent the type are the antitypes, but as these are not the final objective, they also are spoken of as types of the full revelation or antitype. A type is a pictorial copy or representation of Divine realities which are to be afterwards revealed. It is therefore distinctly prophetic, but inasmuch as these realities existed in the Divine mind before the representation of them, they are called in Hebrews 9:24 the antitypes (figures, *ἀντίτυπος*) of the true. The holy places made with hands were the antitypes of the true holy places, namely heaven itself. The only other place in which the word *ἀντίτυπος* is used is 1 Peter 3:21. The ark of Noah was the antitype of the Divine purpose of salvation, and baptism now is the antitype of the death and resurrection of Christ Who effectuated this. Moses alone saw the pattern in the mount, this was the true type of all that he afterwards made; he was shown the original as God saw it. Again the whole system of the Tabernacle made after this pattern, which the epistle to the Hebrews specifically declares to be a heavenly one, became a pattern of things in the heavens.

A *shadow* is the impression formed in the present by a future event, "Shadows of good things to come", but not the very image, not the actuality of the thing itself. A man's shadow is not the very image of himself, though you may recognise him by it.

# Chapter 10: Number

We have already given preliminary consideration to the typical meaning of the materials used in the construction of the Tabernacle, and before proceeding further must now seek to understand the numerical system and standard of measurement which occupy so large a place in the description.

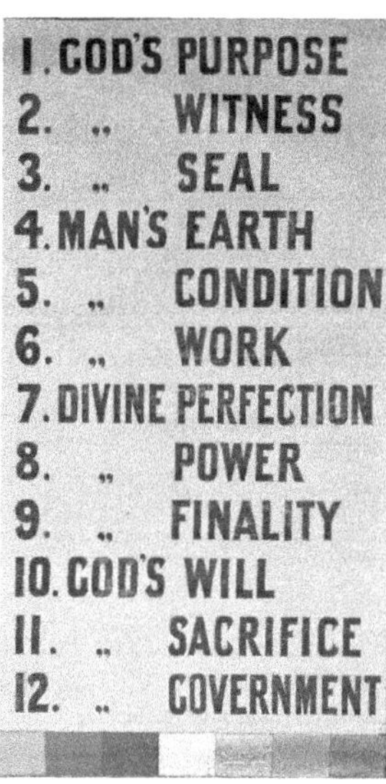


Figure 1: Numbers and Colours in the Tabernacle

The meaning of the numbers is as follows:-

1. God's purpose.
2. God's witness.
3. God's seal.
4. Man's earth or world.
5. Man's capacity & condition, which implies weakness.
6. Man's work.
7. Divine perfection.
8. Divine power, involving resurrection.
9. Divine accomplishment, connected with the oath of God.
10. God's will, and responsibility thereto, of obedience.
11. God's sacrifice: the sin offering number.
12. God's administration or government.

Numeration occupies a large place in Scripture and has great spiritual significance. For many of the thoughts on this subject I am indebted to the writings of F.W. Grant.[11]

### ONE

This number has for its fundamental idea the exclusion of difference.

a. It excludes all other; "The Lord our God is one Lord." It speaks thus of *sufficiency* which *needs*

11 F. W. Grant, *The Numerical Structure of Scripture, a Seal upon its Perfect Inspiration and a Divinely Given Help to its Right Interpretation*, New York City: Loixeaux Brothers, 1887.

no other, and of *independency* which *admits* no other.

b. It excludes external difference, therefore speaks of *concord* and *peace.*

c. It excludes internal difference; "God is one". "The dream is one." The Trinity is a *unity*: Father, Son and Spirit in perfect harmony of parts and attributes, hence absolute righteousness.

d. As an ordinal number; the first, the beginning; in the highest way it speaks of God, and hence connotes Headship, precedence in thought and sovereignty in will, purpose.

The first implies cause. It is the name God claims as His — "I am the First", "The Alpha", and this implies His being the cause of all else. "Out of nothing, nothing can come", assures us that the great First of all must be the Originator of all.

A cause or energy implies power or motion and the effect or phenomena produced demonstrates the perfect, yea, almighty power of the energy which produces it (Romans 1:20).

The highest cause we know lies in will. "I will" would have no meaning apart from the consciousness of power, therefore God only can say "I will" absolutely. If I say "I will", I may through bodily weakness be unable to execute my purpose, still this very fact distinguishes the person who says "I will" from the outer machinery of flesh which it ought to control but cannot. With God there is no "cannot". "He worketh all things after the counsel of His own will" (Ephesians 1:11). It is the highest because it is purposeful. Thus, in the number one, we have a fundamental conception of Deity, namely, a supreme will, intelligent, purposeful, acting in power, and thus the all-sufficient will cause of the universe. Again God must needs be a "living God" and this implies personality, individuality, such for example as the self-contained living thing in Nature is individual. Life and person at least express the unity which plainly enters the thought of God. Person leads us on to the unity of consciousness; all the changes which the years make in our bodies leave us the same persons as before, we have not ourselves changed with the lapse of time, though it is said that our bodies have changed seven times in the course of fifty years. This thought of unchanging person in the creature leads on to God the Unchangeable, and so the Eternal.

There is another unity which fittingly belongs to God, fragmentary in man, perfect in Him: moral unity, namely, a character of consistent harmony in all His attributes, in which there is nothing that is out of proportion, or contradictory, nothing defective nor discordant. Self-consistency in all positions is only possible to perfect goodness, and this is the full blessedness of God. In conclusion, God is one, there is none other, and none to dispute His absolute sway.

## Two

If two different persons agree in testimony it is conclusive. To second a person or something said is to confirm, succour, or help.

Two is also the number that divides, and the truth of a second witness is founded on difference. If the second witness only repeats the testimony, and also if he uses the words of the first witness, instead of producing confidence he destroys it. We need the evidence of two persons for the confirmation of a point in question, but with a diversity of interest, feelings and general outlook. Each of our eyes views an object from a different angle, together they concur in giving it solidity, actuality.

In the Godhead the Son is the second person, in manhood He is the Second Man. Two natures far apart brought into a complete witness to the perfection of Him Who came to do His will alone. He is therefore the True Witness, the expression of the Unseen, the Image of the Invisible. He is God manifest, made tangible, evident, seen and heard (1 John 1). He is God's witness of Himself, for all the fullness was pleased to dwell in Him. Finally He is the appointed divider and judge of all, and this because He has come into death, the division of soul and body.

## Three

Only three modes of extension or dimension actually exist in the things our senses observe, and three alone are possible to thought: length, breadth and height or thickness. Any solid, tangible reality must have the third dimension. Thus the number three signifies a cube.

Three is ideally the great producer. A plan is in two dimensions, it needs a third in actual construction to give it solidity, actuality. No one can live in a plan, a house must be built to it. Two straight lines cannot enclose a space, a third is necessary, and this gives the idea of enclosing, setting apart. The Holy Spirit is the third person of the Trinity, without Him we could not speak of the Triune God.[12] It is He who gives effect to, and reproduces, the personality and character of God, revealed in the Person of the Son.

---

12 The Triune God is not represented by 1+1+1 which equals 3, but by 1×1×1 which equal 1.

Three is the number of the Divine name, thus:–

| | |
|---|---|
| The God of Abraham: | The God of *purpose* and *promise.* |
| The God of Isaac: | The God of *power* and *resurrection.* |
| The God of Jacob: | The God of *grace.* |

The three parables of Luke 15 also set forth the actings of God: Father, Son and Spirit. The three numbers 1, 2, 3, maintain their integrity, they bear the stamp of the Divine. They are all primes incapable of true division. The sanctuary is a cube, 10 cubits in the Tabernacle; 20 in the temple; and also the city (Revelation 21), 12,000 furlongs.

The triangle is a mathematical unity and is frequently used as a symbol of the Divine Trinity, which truth underlies the '*kosmos*' of which Man is the created head, his body carrying upon it the sign of the Divine claim. Three is stamped upon creation in many ways: in the vegetable world as bud, flower and fruit; in the animal, by head, thorax and abdomen. The three parts of the Tabernacle were holy place, holy and holiest. Three heavens are spoken of, and the structure of the prophet Isaiah consists largely of threes, the Divine seal upon the prophetic word.

Blue, Red and Yellow seen in the spectrum form a trinity of radiant energy, power, heat & light. Green, Orange, Purple and Violet are combinations of these, the whole together forming the visible white light. Christ is the image of the invisible to mortal eyes, the spectrum being the symbol of His glory manifested, as in the rainbow; whilst at the crimson end are the invisible heat rays, warming and vivifying, an apt symbol of the Father; and beyond the visible at the violet end are the unseen actinic power rays searching, penetrating, transforming, a no less apt symbol of the Spirit's energy.

Truth, like light, is also a unity in three-fold expression:–

1. God is true in His moral nature, absolutely consistent with Himself and eternally so.

2. Christ is true; the two-fold witness, God and Man, entirely competent, without admixture, trustworthy.

3. The Spirit is truth; the final seal, holy; holiness agreeing with this, namely, viewing things as they are in the sight of God, thinking His thoughts, accepting things at their true value, all of which involves the practice of righteousness, and separation from unrighteousness. Compare 'Holiness of truth' (Ephesians 4:24, R.V.).

Love, again like light and truth, is a unity in a three-fold way:–

1. Love existing eternally in the Divine nature.

2. Love reconciling the division made by evil.

3. Love perfected in the soul of man (1 John 4:6).

## Four

This number can be formed in two ways:–

3 + 1 significant of Divine sovereignty.

2 × 2 significant of evil and separation.

It is the earth number. We speak of the four corners of the earth, showing earthly completeness and universality; four winds of heaven expressive of various and opposing influences of which earth is the scene.

The fourth book of Scripture presents the walk of the people of God on earth. Foursquare, 2 squared, always has reference to material creation pertaining to the earth, things terrestrial, namely, things under the sun. The altar was foursquare, the sacrifice exhibited on earth; the city lieth foursquare, showing the administration exercised on earth.

Four Gentile empires exercise sovereignty over the earth; four living creatures symbolise the execution of the will of God on earth. It was on the fourth day that lights were set in the firmament to give light upon the earth, and to rule over the day and night.

### Five

This is the number of man's condition under the government of God. The mark of it is upon his hand, 5 fingers, that he should do His work; and upon his foot that he should walk in His ways, 5 toes; and these being doubled (10) adds the thought of governmental direction. Man has also five senses by which he makes contact with external conditions. We may note the five points by which man is identified with, and able to aid and serve his fellows, in the case of Elisha and the child (2 Kings 4:34), two hands, two eyes, one mouth. This leads on to the thought of grace which was characteristic of Elisha. Five denotes Divine grace for Christ came into man's condition. Five is 1 + 4, "*I* came into the *world*." Five is the leading factor in the Tabernacle measurements. In the ceremonies relating to the consecration of the priests and the cleansing of the leper, blood and oil were put upon:–

- *The ear*, representing the five senses, the avenues of perception by which man can be appealed to, hearing, seeing, tasting, feeling and smelling.

- *The hand*, expressive of action. It is the sign that man is the vice-regent of God, but his power lies in dependence, not like Divine power, simple and without effort, but a co-operation of forces. Four fingers helped by thumb, with two hands assisting one another, $(4 + 1) \times 2$ is 10. This is the number of natural responsibility, for this reason we have the expressions "made with hands", "done by hand". When man's actions and ways are under God's control he fulfils his responsibility, but this was perfectly seen only in Christ.
- *The foot.* The same may be said of the foot upon which the numbers 5 and 10 are again expressed, conveying the thought of responsibility in walk. Five exhortations to walk suitably to God are found in the Epistle to the Ephesians.

There are 5 books in the Pentateuch.

There are 5 books of poetry in the Old Testament.

There are 5 books which compose the book of Psalms.

There are 5 books of major prophets in the Old Testament.

There are 5 books of history in the New Testament.

## Six

This is the number signifying work. Man was created on the sixth day, the hours of Man's day are a multiple of six: 12 and 24. It is thus the number of God's work in creation, and of man's work-day week, "Six days shalt thou labour and do all thy work." Work may be viewed from the point of view of evil, as we find it in the number of the beast in three successive higher powers, 666. It is the work of evil fully displayed in the number of a man impiously aspiring to be as God. In Psalm 10, the arrangement of which, with Psalm 9, is alphabetical, six letters (*mem* to *tzaddi*) are omitted in the verses 3-11 which describe this wicked one. Goliath's height was six cubits and one of his race had six fingers and six toes. Nebuchadnezzar's image was 60 cubits high and six broad. Thus six, is the number of work either good or evil, either of God, man or Satan. It is the witness of man's opposition to God, as Athaliah usurped the throne of Judah for six years; and it is the witness of God's work on behalf of man. The darkness of the cross began at the sixth hour (work) and ended at the ninth (seal).

Six is the first perfect number; namely, the sum of its divisors, omitting itself, equals six. 1 + 2 + 3 equals six. The next perfect number is 28. The factors of these indicate the perfect manifestation of good and evil, whether in Christ or Antichrist.

### SEVEN

The number of Divine perfection. In a good sense its meaning is perfect Divine accomplishment, but it may be applied to evil in the sense of completeness. 7 and 12 are both formed from the combination of 4 and 3, in the case of 7 they are added, 4 + 3, that is Divine manifestation in man's world; in the case of 12, 4 × 3, there is active Divine energy laying hold of man's world and forming in it a perfect manifestation of grace. Seven is of very frequent use in Scripture and especially so in the book of the Revelation, which sets forth the complete summing up of the great issues of good and evil. The numerical value of the letters of the Greek word '*stauros*' ('cross') is 777. In the animal world and also in man the periods of incubation and gestation are nearly always multiples of seven, and this law of completion in weeks is evident in the Scriptures as well. In Hebrew the same word is used for week as for seven, the term 'week' simply meaning a period divided into seven parts. Thus we find:–

| | |
|---|---|
| The week of days | Genesis 2:2-3; Exodus 20:8-11. |
| The week of weeks | Pentecost (Leviticus 23:15-22). |
| The week of months | The sacred portion of the Jewish year ordained for religious ceremonies occupied the first seven months of the year (Leviticus 23) |
| The week of years | Sabbatic year law (Leviticus 25:1-7). |
| The week of weeks of years | The Jubilee (Leviticus 25:8-22). |
| The week of seven decades | 490 (Daniel 9). |
| The week of one decade | 70: The period of human life (Psalm 90:10). |

The law of septiform periodicy is engraven widely and deeply on the animal creation, the Scriptures of truth, and the human family, and it may be that the period of this world's history will be a seven of millenniums, but God only knows the secret as to when the last of these shall be commenced.

> "Only 7 combines these two peculiarities within the limits of 1 to 10, namely, multiplication does not produce it, nor does it

produce any number within these limits by multiplication. It is therefore called the 'virgin number'. In the dual or binary system 111 = 7, thus $2^2 + 2^1 + 2^0 = 7$ and every seventh number thus reached is always a square or a cube. For example 1, 2, 4, 8, 16, 32, 64, this seventh number is the square of 8 and the cube of 4. In Revelation 21 the city, in which is summed up the completion and repose of the labour of God, is both foursquare and a cube" (H.J.Vine {edited}).[13]

## EIGHT

This number is connected with power evidenced by the fact of resurrection. It is a new beginning, and on the first day of the week our Lord rose from the dead. The connection of this fact with power is seen in Ephesians 1:19-20. The over-passing of the week of time brings in eternity as symbolized by the eighth day of the Feast of Tabernacles. It may rightly be called the Dominical Number[14] for it or its multiples are impressed upon the numerical values of the Lord's names and titles.

| | | | | |
|---|---|---|---|---|
| Jesus | *Ἰησοῦς* | 888 | 800 + 80 + 8 | |
| Christ | *Χριστός* | 1480 | 8 × 185 | |
| Saviour | *Σωτήρ* | 1408 | 8 × 176 | $8^2 \times 22$ |
| Messiah | *Μεσσίας* | 656 | 8 × 82 | |
| Lord | *Κύριος* | 800 | 8 × 100 | |

13 H.J.Vine, *Precious Stones of Scripture: The Chrysolite* in *Scripture Truth*, Volume 8, page 214, 1916.

14 E.W.Bullinger, *Number in Scripture: Its Supernatural Design and Spiritual Significance*, London: Eyre and Spottiswoode, 1894, pages 203-4.

Eight is sometimes applied to evil as a last state as in the case of the seven spirits plus one in Matthew 12:45, and the eighth head of the beast (Revelation 17:11.).

## Nine

This is the Divine number squared: 3 × 3. It is never found in the Tabernacle measurements. It expresses finality and is connected with the oath of God, "When He could swear by no greater He sware by Himself." So it is never connected which that which is temporary and passing, such as types and shadows.[15]

The indication of finality which belongs to it is seen in the following incidents:–

- It was in the 9th year of Zedekiah that Jerusalem was besieged by Nebuchadnezzar (2 Kings 25:1).
- On the 9th day of the month Jerusalem was taken (2 Kings 25:3-4).
- It was at the 9th hour Jesus cried with a loud voice, "It is finished" ({Matthew 27:46-50, Mark 15:34-37; John 19:30}, Luke 23:44-46).
- It was at the 9th hour that Cornelius saw the vision (Acts 10:30).
- It was in the 9th month Jehoiakim burned the roll (Jeremiah 36:22).

Nine has this remarkable characteristic, that the digits which compose the result of its multiplication, if added together always amount to 9 or its multiples.

9 × 3 = 27, 2 + 7 = 9.

2354 × 9 = 21186, sum of digits = 18.

987435 × 9 = 8886915, sum of digits = 45; etc.

[15] Incidentally it may be remarked that the number of articles of priestly attire worn by the High Priest was nine.

In this unfailing recurrence is the indication that whatever extension there may be of the Divine action, it ever glorifies itself, and its sum can never be otherwise than its own expression.

### TEN

The number of responsibility to God's government: 5 × 2. The ten fingers are man's capacity for action, his ten toes are his competence for an upright walk. But the measure of capacity is that of responsibility, and the measure of this responsibility is that of judgment or reward. This is seen in:–

- The 10 words of the Law.
- the 10th was the amount of the tithe.
- 10 pounds was the entrusted deposit in Luke 19.
- The millennial descriptions in Ezekiel 45 & 48, are multiples of 10.

### ELEVEN

This is the number of sacrifice, standing between ten, which speaks of responsibility, and twelve which represents the administration of blessing. It is the sin offering number, for on eleven different occasions one kid of the goats for a sin offering was presented. Eleven curtains of goats' hair, the animal of the sin offering, formed the tent of the Tabernacle. Apart from sacrifice in relation to sin, there can be no blessing for man or glory brought to God.

Eleven being the fifth prime number adds the thought that it was by One in man's condition that the sacrifice was offered. "Since by man came death, by man came also the resurrection from the dead." Being a prime it can only be formed by addition and in five ways by the use of the ten digits which are the foundation upon which number depends:

6 + 5; 7 + 4; 8 + 3; 9 + 2; 10 + 1.

In this is indicated the fundamental character of the sacrifice by which all things are reckoned.

## TWELVE

This number is connected with things which have to do with government and administration, such as twelve tribes, twelve patriarchs, twelve apostles and measurements of time. It is formed by the multiplication of 4 and 3, and not simply by addition as 7 = 4 + 3. It is only in the relation of the two numbers that 7 and 12 differ. The number of the earth and that of Divine manifestation characterise it, but these are not side by side merely as in the number 7, not simply rest but active energy, multiplication, God laying hold of the earth of His creation and transforming it. Thus 12 is the number of manifest sovereignty. This is expressed in the city of Revelation 21 — 12 foundations, 12 gates of pearl, length, breadth, height 12,000 furlongs, wall 144 cubits, the tree of life with 12 manner of fruits 12 times in the year.

## OTHER NUMBERS IN SCRIPTURE

— are formed from a combination of these, as 40, the probation number of testing on earth regarding responsibility, 10 × 4. 17 denotes a combination of responsibility and perfection and is the seventh prime number, while 13 is the sixth, the first mention of 13 being in connection with rebellion (Genesis 14:4).

The four numbers 3 × 7 × 10 × 12 = 2520 which represents the number of days in 7 prophetic years of 360 days. It is in itself a remarkable number for it is the

L.C.M. {Least (or Lowest) Common Multiple} of the digits 1 to 10, each of which will divide it without a remainder, thus:

1 is contained in it 2520 times, no remainder.

2 is contained in it 1260 times, no remainder.

3 is contained in it 840 times, no remainder.

4 is contained in it 630 times, no remainder.

5 is contained in it 504 times, no remainder.

6 is contained in it 420 times, no remainder.

7 is contained in it 360 times, no remainder.

8 is contained in it 315 times, no remainder.

9 is contained in it 280 times, no remainder.

10 is contained in it 252 times, no remainder.

2520 is the number of days during which the madness of Nebuchadnezzar continued: 7 years or times. This is representative of the last seven years of the Times of the Gentiles, the season of the apostacy, when the pride of man will assume dominion over the authority of God.

The significance of a number when simple equals the fact presented. When squared there is in addition the Divine Witness, God's Word. When cubed there is further the Divine seal, God's oath; these last being the two immutable things, concerning which no change can take place.

## Chapter 11: The Measurements

These we must now consider. The measurements of the Tabernacle are after the *cubit*, and in order to understand the symbolism this unit must be retained in the mind. The actual measure, when reduced to inches, has been variously estimated. Both the Babylonians and the Greeks had two cubits in use, the *middling*, equal to 18.205 English inches, and the *royal*, 20½ inches. So amongst the Hebrews there was the cubit "after the cubit of a man" (Deuteronomy 3:11), and the cubit used in Ezekiel's vision equal to "a cubit and a hand-breadth", 22½ inches (chapters 40:5 and 43:13).

The latter seems to have been in use after the captivity, the first or shorter cubit being alluded to in 2 Chronicles 3:3. The early measures of length among men were generally derived from the human frame and for this reason the cubit or *'ammah'* (Hebrew) measuring 18 inches seems to be the most appropriate as it approximates to the normal height of a man. From the crown of the head to the soles of the feet is 6 feet or 4 cubits. With the arms extended, the measure from the tip of each middle finger is the same as the height;

bringing the tips of the fingers together upon the breast, the measure from elbow to elbow is 2 cubits or 3 feet, which makes the length of the forearm from finger tip to elbow 1 cubit or 18 inches. The half cubit, or span is the distance from the thumb to the little finger when the hand is spread, namely 9 inches. This again is divided into 2 handbreadths of 4½ inches or ¼ cubit. One fifth of this or 'finger' was the smallest measure in use (Jeremiah 52:21), but this does not occur in the Tabernacle. Symbolically the measure of a man is the measure of the stature of the fulness of Christ. He is the standard by which God measures all things, and the measurements of the Tabernacle are designed for the expression of this.

The larger cubit of Ezekiel's vision, 22½ inches, would appear to express expansion, display, as suitable to a scene of glory.

## Chapter 12: The Specification

There are five descriptions of the Tabernacle in the book of Exodus, the order differing in each case.

The first, chapters 25:1 to 30:38, is the original specification given by God to Moses in the Mount. In this the person of Christ is the leading thought, and things connected with His work, character, testimony and priesthood.

The second, chapters 36:8 to 39:32, gives the detail of the construction, and in this the order is different from the first, the mediatorial glories of Christ being prominent and His personal excellence as Mediator. Then the means by which the new covenant is established, namely death, followed by the things which concern the consequent moral character of those who come under the new covenant and the priestly family.

The third, chapter 39:33-43, relates to the presentation of the finished work, corresponding in type to Christ risen.

The fourth, chapter 40:1-16, having reference to the anointing, would answer to the ascension of Christ.

"God hath made that same Jesus, whom ye have crucified, both Lord and Christ" {Acts 2:36}.

The fifth, chapter 40:17-38, relates to the coming glory and looks forward to the glorious day when Christ shall sit as priest upon His throne, and Jerusalem be 'Jehovah Shammah' {'The Lord is there", Ezekiel 48:35}.

The five descriptions are added for comparison.

| **1 Exodus 25:1 to 30:38** | **2 Exodus 36:8 to 39:32** | **3 Exodus 39:33-43** | **4 Exodus 40:1-16** | **5 Exodus 40:17-38** |
|---|---|---|---|---|
| Ark | Curtains | Curtains | Boards | Boards |
| Table | Tent | Tent | Curtains | Tent |
| Lampstand | Coverings | Boards | Tent | Curtains |
| Curtains | Boards | Coverings | Ark | Coverings |
| Tent | Vail | Vail | Vail | Ark |
| Coverings | Door | Ark | Table | Vail |
| Boards | Ark | Table | Lampstand | Table |
| Vail | Table | Lampstand | Incense Altar | Lampstand |
| Door | Lampstand | Incense Altar | Door | Incense Altar |
| Altar | Incense Altar | Ointment | Altar | Incense |
| Court | Ointment | Incense | Laver | Altar |
| Robes | Incense | Door | Court | Laver |
| Anointing | Altar | Altar | Ointment | Court |
| Incense Altar | Laver | Laver | Robes | |
| Laver | Court | Court | | |
| Ointment | Robes | Robes | | |
| Incense | | | | |

## Chapter 13: The Way of Approach

The desire of God is to have a people near to Himself, and with that in view the series of types in Exodus, from Egypt to the Ark of the Covenant in the Holiest, may be read as indicating a straight line of approach, answering in reality to the new and living way (Hebrews 10:20).

*Justification* is shown in the Passover.

*Separation* to God in the Red Sea.

*Condemnation* of sin in the Brazen Serpent.

*Emancipation* is seen in the Jordan.

*Imputation* is seen in the Sin-Offering.

In the faith of these the next thing is approach, The Gate.

*Acceptation* is evident in the Brazen Altar.

*Sanctification* is evident in the Laver.

Then access is reached in the Door of the Tabernacle.

*Presentation* follows in the Table of Shewbread.

*Illumination* follows in the Lampstand.

And thus boldness of entrance through the Vail into the Holiest of all to find all that the blood of Jesus is for God; and finally:

*Manifestation* in the Ark of the Covenant.

Reversing the order, the Tabernacle arrangement presents God reaching out to the sinner. God is seen looking out from the Ark, through the Vail, the flesh of Christ, "The Word became flesh". He is seen in the presentation of grace in the Incense altar; by the right hand of power revealing Himself by the light of the Lampstand; by His left hand of love providing the bread of life as seen in the Table and its loaves; and outwards, between those outstretched hands, is the witness of death in the Altar and Laver, the utmost length to which love could go. "God so loved the world that He gave His only begotten Son". It is this that has provided the gate of approach.

# Part 2:
# The Tabernacle

## Chapter 14: Instruction

The teaching of the *Tabernacle* may be viewed in three ways. It foreshadows:–

1. A peerless person.
2. A privileged people.
3. A purchased possession.

Pre-eminently it sets forth Christ in His person, work and present position. It is the type of a peerless person, and on account of such an one having been revealed, it is easier to understand its details as the Hebrews' epistle shows.

*Solomon's Temple*, constructed in the land, foreshadowed the millennial glory of a reigning Christ with God's family. It was the symbol therefore of a privileged people, and no doubt this was in our Lord's mind when He said, "In My Father's house are many abiding places", referring to the Temple chambers (1 Kings 6:5-10).

When *Ezekiel's Temple* shall be constructed by Christ in the Millennium it will anticipate Eternity, when God will be all in all: the pattern of a purchased possession.

We shall see in the vessels or furniture of the Tabernacle the *Offices* of Christ; in the fabrics His *Character*; in the structure His personal *Glory*, and in the priestly robes His *Present Service*.

Secondly, we shall see in the structure a privileged people who form the house of God, His habitation; and in the priestly family His worshippers.

Thirdly, there are the good things to come which the day of Christ will display, these are seen in the general arrangement:

In relation to heaven:–

1. The Ark, God's throne = God the centre and judge of all.
2. The Holiest = heaven itself. The Father's house, the place of the Church.
3. The Holy = The heavenlies. Christ displayed in Old Testament saints.
4. The Holy place = The created heavens, the place of sacrifice.

In relation to earth:–

5. The camp of Levi = Jerusalem, the place of government.
6. The camp of 12 tribes = Israel's inheritance, the land of promise.
7. The nations around = Gentiles blessed under Christ.

The whole forms a framework of the world to come.

To sum up before proceeding to the description of the detail of the various parts, we have in the Tabernacle a figure of the heavens:

1. The Court;
2. The Holy;
3. The Holiest.

On the great Day of Atonement the priest passed through the first and second into the third, the scene of the immediate presence of God. There is an allusion to the significance of this in Hebrews 4:14. "We have a great High Priest that is passed through the heavens".

Paul also speaks of being caught up into Paradise, the third heaven (2 Corinthians 12:2, 4).

In Acts 7:44 Stephen states the fact that the Tabernacle had been made as God appointed according to the fashion He had shown to Moses. What was it then that Jehovah showed Moses? In Hebrews 8:5 we are told that the priests served "unto the example and shadow of heavenly things, as Moses was admonished of God when he was about to make the Tabernacle: for, See, saith He, that thou make all things according to the pattern showed to thee in the Mount." In verse 2 the Tabernacle is said to be a shadow "of the true Tabernacle, which the Lord pitched, and not man"; and in chapter 9:8 that the Holy Spirit by it signified "that the way into the Holiest of all was not yet made manifest". In verse 9 we are told that it was "a figure for the time then present", but verse 11 {tells us} that when Christ came He would exercise His priesthood in "a greater and more perfect tabernacle not made with hands". Then the chapter proceeds to contrast the earthly building with the heavenly realities after the pattern of which it had been made.

Then again "Christ is not entered into the holy places made by hands, which are the figures of the true, but into heaven itself" (Hebrews 9:24).

From the foregoing we may gather in answer to our question that God caused to pass before the vision of Moses the great realities of Christ's person and work, upon which the full millennial blessing and Divine purpose for Israel depend. The great secret of the calling of the Church and her association with Christ in His reign, was hidden from him, the time when this was to be revealed had not come (Ephesians 3:5; Colossians 1:26).

Let us then measure the pattern, for thereby much will be conveyed to our souls of His glory Who will head up in Himself the secret things of God as well as those revealed to His servant Moses. Enlightened by the Spirit of God we may behold in these types, as in a mirror, the glory of the Lord, anticipating that glad day when the vail shall be taken from the heart of Israel and they shall see Him in the Scriptures of Truth, Whose name is Wonderful, and shall look upon Him Whom they have pierced.

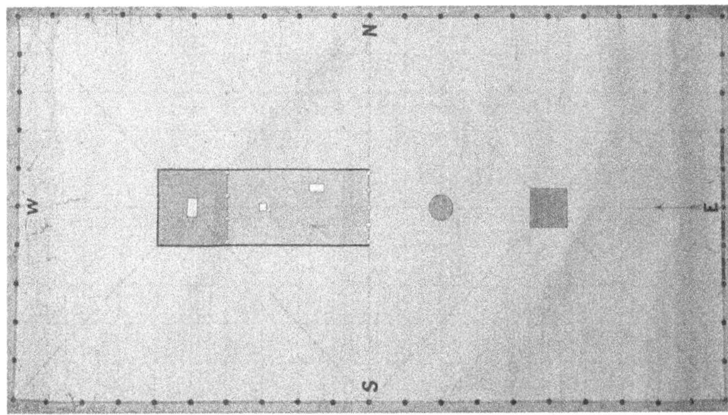


Figure 2: Plan of the Tabernacle

## Chapter 15:
## The Court

EXODUS 27:9-19; EXODUS 38:9-20, 28, 31.

The Court of the Tabernacle was an enclosure defined by curtains of fine white linen, and must have presented a marked contrast to the dark tents which composed the camp of Israel, which were like the Bedouin tents in use at the present day. There may be an allusion to this contrast in Song of Solomon 1:5. The bride says, "I am black", the bridegroom replies, "But comely". She says, "As the tents of Kedar", and he says, "As the curtains of Solomon".

The length of the Court was 100 cubits and the breadth 50 cubits. In Exodus 27:18 the breadth is spoken of as 50 × 50 everywhere (Authorized Version margin) that is, it is viewed as consisting of two squares of 50 cubits each (see diagram). In the centre of the first square was the altar, in the centre of the second was the ark (compare Ezekiel 40:47). The sufferings of Christ (altar) and the glory that should follow (ark) are the two centres (*foci*) around which the great ellipse of God's purposes in Christ revolves, all things on earth and in heaven being summed up in Him. The altar was fulfilled

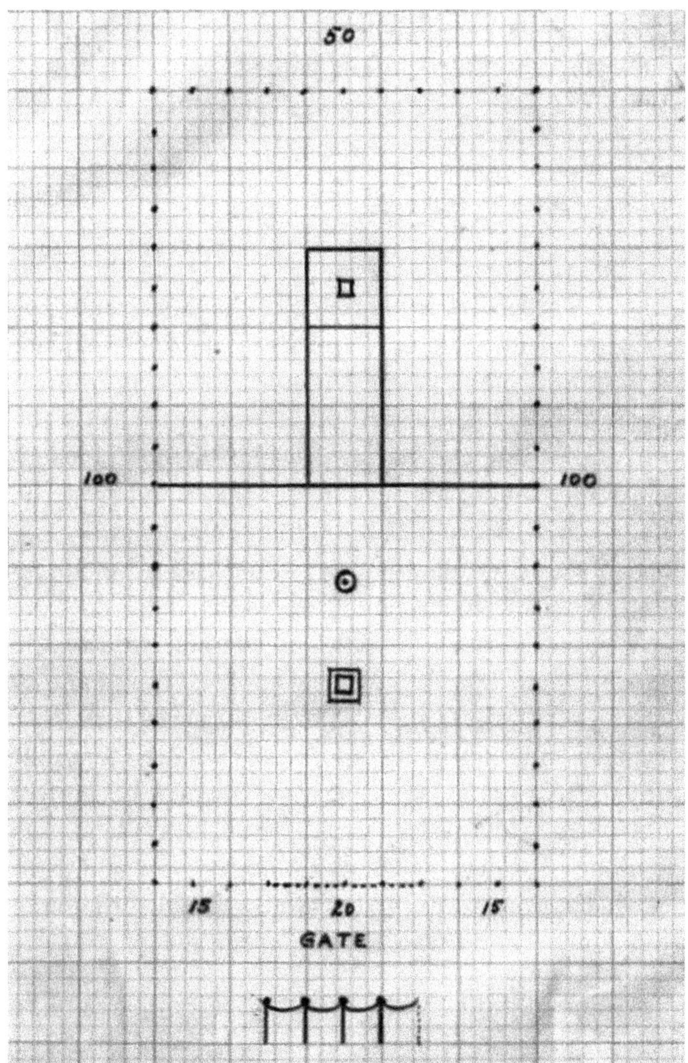


Figure 3: Plan of the Court

on earth, the ark is His glory in heaven. The number 5 and its multiples govern the Tabernacle measurements. 100 cubits tell of God's witness that every responsibility was perfectly fulfilled in His pathway; $10 \times 10 = 100$, while $5 \times 10 = 50$ emphasizes the fact that it was in man's capacity that He did so.

## The Linen Curtains

Fine linen curtains separated the court from the camp without. These were supported by 60 pillars arranged as in Figure 3. Each of these pillars supported 5 square cubits of fine linen, making the court 100 cubits long on the south side, the same on the north, 50 cubits on the west, and on the east 50 divided into three, 15 plus 15 equals 30 of linen, on each side of the hanging for the gate which measured 20 cubits. The total length of the linen curtains, minus the gate, would therefore be 280 cubits. The fine twined linen or byssus, represents the perfect righteousness which was characteristic of the pathway of our Lord in which no spot was found and in which every word and act was in perfect relation (twined), not consisting simply of isolated acts, but presenting from every aspect the display of perfect righteousness in perfect unity. The 119th Psalm sets forth how, through the whole alphabet of life, all was in perfect accord with the will of God, and it was the same from whichever point of the compass it was viewed.

The Court standing in the midst of the camp exhibited the only standard of righteousness which God can approve, and this became a barrier which excluded all else. The height of the linen curtains was 5 cubits, one cubit higher than the height of a man, 4 cubits; for the life of such an one as the Son of God was and is far above the attainment of man's natural condition. With such a standard the imitation of Christ is an impossibility to the Adam race, hence when man attempts this he must of necessity lower the perfect standard to his own conception, that he may flatter himself that he has attained it. The square of 5 cubits, $5^2$, indicates God's witness or approval, and the total length of 280 cubits — 7 × 4 × 10 — adds the thought of perfection seen in Christ in man's world, in which all others have sinned and come short of the glory of God. Had the linen in its purity entirely surrounded the court, there would have been no approach to God, but in the centre of the east side a gate was provided of fine linen like the rest, for there can be no abatement of righteousness, but upon this there was needlework of blue, purple and scarlet, colours which symbolize the mediatorial glories of Christ, and upon this there was the splash of blood (Hebrews 9:21), for it is through death that the way has been opened, and that for the whole world, hence the gate hung upon four pillars. These may suggest the four Gospels. The area of the gate was 100 square cubits — 20 × 5 — the same as the area of the door and the vail — 10 × 10 — in each case speaking of responsibility fulfilled and Divinely attested, but in the gate with the further thought of extension world-wide.

*Needlework* means embroidered on one side, presentation; whilst *cunning work* refers to that which is intrinsic, wrought through, alike on both sides.

The sinless person to whom all the glory belonged has died and through His death the way to God has been opened. It is this that the Court so eloquently sets forth, and for this reason all the vessels belonging to it were of copper, the fire-enduring metal. Altar, Laver, Sockets, Pins and Utensils were of the same (chapters 27:19 and

38:20). All was typical of the great truth of Divine righteousness which is the foundation and support of all approach to God. The teaching of the Court would correspond to that of the epistle to the Romans in which this fundamental principle is insisted on. It is demanded, fulfilled, declared, reckoned, maintained, is triumphant, and shall be finally exhibited. The righteousness of God is God's perfect consistency with all that He is in nature and character, and the glory of the Gospel is that every attribute of God has been brought into perfect adjustment and unity of action by Him Who knew no sin, but was made sin for us upon the Cross. The great result is that all who believe in Him become the righteousness of God in Him, Who is the eternal witness and exhibition of God's character. Every attribute is seen in harmonious working in regard to the absolute judgment of sin and in respect of the exceeding riches of His grace. On this is based the great privilege of Christian fellowship. The Court was where the Levites congregated, where they met each other, and the one fellowship of Jesus Christ our Lord would correspond to this. It is a fellowship into which we have come by the door; in which Christ is our separation from the world, and where our occupation and communion is with His death — the Altar and the Laver (1 Corinthians 10:16-17).

### The Pillars

The curtains of the Court were supported by 60 pillars. We are not distinctly told the material of which these were made. Exodus 27:10 reads in the Authorized Version, "The twenty pillars thereof and their twenty sockets (shall be of) brass", but there is no verb in the original and brass may refer to the sockets alone. The Septuagint reads, "Their pillars twenty and twenty brazen sockets". Josephus says that the pillars were brass. Ridout agrees with this, and so does F. W. Grant, but admits that the amount of brass spoken of in chapter 38:29, seventy talents, would appear to be insufficient to make such pillars with the other things. Keil takes it for granted that the pillars were of acacia wood, and I agree with this latter and for this reason. Acacia (shittim wood) {see page 60} is a symbol of the holy humanity of our Lord Jesus Christ, and only such an One could support the spotless righteousness which marked His life. If this be so, the pillars would be the only uncovered wood in the Tabernacle, and thus in a peculiar way emphasize "The man Christ Jesus". We shall find in the Tabernacle description many omissions regarding size, weight, material, etc. and where this is so, it indicates that the thing typified is inscrutable to the human mind and known alone to God. This is so in the case of the humanity of Our Lord. "The first man is of the earth earthy, the second man is out of heaven" (1 Corinthians 15:47). As another has said, "He was as much a man as I am, but not such a man as I am", and this apart from the question of being sinless, for Adam was this, but being of the earth had the capacity of sinning, but Christ, as to moral being entirely from heaven, was incapable of sin (compare 1 John 3:9).

Each pillar rested upon a socket of copper, expressive of that character of Divine righteousness which the Altar, made of the same material, alone could supply. The capitals of silver which crowned each pillar spoke of the price of redemption; and the fillets[16], or rather

16 'Fillets' from primitive root *chashaq* 'to cling', i.e. 'to join'
*piel* 'fillet' Exodus 38:28 active
*pual* 'filleted' Exodus 27:17 & 38:17 passive
pass.part. *chashuqim* = attached, i.e. a fence, rail or connecting rod.

connecting rods, joined the pillars together, showing the oneness of the work.

Then the hooks by which the curtains were suspended clearly speak of the dependence of Him Who said, "Preserve Me, O God, for in Thee do I put My trust". Only the Son of God perfect in man's true place could sustain righteousness in relation to redemption.

Besides this each pillar was strongly supported by cords fastened to pins of copper (Numbers 4:32), typical of the stability which was so markedly characteristic of the path of our Lord. "Because He is at my right hand I shall not be moved" (Psalm 16:8). The word 'pin' (*yathad*) is elsewhere translated 'nail' (Judges 4:21-22; 5:26; Isaiah 33:20; 54:2); compare also Isaiah 22:20-25, where the word translated 'sure' has the same derivation as the Hebrew word '*amen*'.

Christ is the security of all God's counsels of love, mercy and blessing, the cord connecting these with earth. It is not stated of what material the cords, which are not mentioned until Numbers 4:32, were made, probably blue, purple, scarlet and linen. In the wilderness where faith is tested, it is necessary that we should be reminded of the stability of Christ, so that leaning upon His unchangeableness we may abide unshaken. Hence in the wilderness epistle, that to the Hebrews, in the first and last chapters Christ is presented as 'The Same'. Notwithstanding the fact that He was amidst the desolateness and ruin of this wilderness world, He maintained uninterrupted intercourse with the redemptive purpose of God, the silver capitals, and through this unceasing blessings flow down to us from Him.

Silver is typical of redemption. Every man in Israel from 20 years old and upwards had to give a *bekah* or half shekel as ransom money. The amount thus obtained amounted to 100 talents, and 1775 shekels. The 100 talents[17] were used in the foundation of the Tabernacle, and the remainder for the capitals, connecting rods and hooks of the pillars of the Court (Exodus 38:28).

The fine linen hanging from the silver hooks and rods, shows the inseparable connection which exists between Christ our righteousness and Christ our redemption. To say that we are made righteous by His life of obedience loosens the hangings from the silver hooks. Everything that touched the earth in the Court of the Tabernacle was of copper. The foundation of all approach to God must be His righteous judgment of sin, hence we shall see, that the Altar is of the same. The length of the linen curtains exclusive of the gate was 280 cubits — 7 × 40, perfection manifested by testing. The number of the pillars was 60 — 10 × 6 — expressive of the work in which every responsibility was fulfilled and the work of God completed. “I have finished the work that Thou gavest Me to do.” The binding of the whole enclosure together by silver rods gives the thought of the unity of purpose that characterised our Lord in His ministry. “I came not to do Mine own will, but the will of Him that sent Me.” It is this redemption work that has provided a gate, a way of approach to God.

## The Gate

### The Curtain of the Gate

This was 20 cubits wide, suspended on 4 pillars of the Court at the eastern end. It was wrought with

[17] *kikkar*: a talent, {equal to 50 *minas* or 3,000 *shekels*; exact weight in current measures uncertain.}

needlework of blue, purple, scarlet upon the same texture of fine linen which composed the Court. The 20 cubits, which is made up of 2 × 10, would indicate the Divine Witness to the fulfilment of the Divine Will, and its height, like the Court of 5 cubits, that this was done in human condition, whilst its area of 100 square cubits would mark more strongly 20 × 5, the Divine Witness. The four pillars point out the world-wide extent of this witness to all men, as does the extended form likewise indicate readiness to receive all who come by Christ, the Way.

The embroidered colours, the full meaning of which will come before us later in the Tabernacle itself, indicate the heavenly, universal and earthly glories of Christ. Across the Gate was the sprinkling of blood, for the perfect life of Him to Whom these glories belong has been laid down in death, and it is the fact that He so gave Himself for us, that has opened the way of approach to God. The teaching of the Court is this, that apart from His atoning death, Christ's life becomes a barrier. If only such an one can stand in God's holy presence, then every other man is shut out. But there is a gate provided, one and only one, for Christ is the only way of salvation, and none other name under heaven is of any avail.

Four pillars were provided for the gate, though to appearance it was suspended from five. It must however be remembered that each pillar is regarded as supporting its own square of curtain measuring five square cubits, hence four pillars for four squares. The number five is the leading numeral in these types. If the bases of the pillars be joined by lines across the Court and from end to end, (see plan on page 95) the area consisting of 5000 square cubits is composed of squares

Figure 4: General view of the Tabernacle

of 5 × 5 cubits. The approach of God to man has its foundation in the fact that the Word became flesh and tabernacled amongst us. He laid aside the form (*morphos*) (Philippians 2:6-7) belonging to the eternal mystery of the Godhead, without ceasing to be what He ever was and must be, God over all blessed for ever; and which glory was His before the world's foundation, He has now resumed without laying aside the manhood that He took, though now glorified. He it is Who has opened the way, and He alone could do it. By the shedding of His blood, He has opened the way back to the heart of God for ever, for every soul that submits his sinnership to Him.

The four sides of the Court represent the testing of Christ under all circumstances. North and South, 20 pillars, 10 × 2, represent the witness of God to His perfect fulfilment of every responsibility, whether under the sharpness of the north wind of rejection, or the warmth of the south wind of intercourse with those whom the Father had given to Him. Or again, 10 pillars westward, in His maintenance of the rights of God in a world where these were declining to sunset in the thoughts of men. Or yet again in the presentation of the grace of God to sinners, as on the east side, for here the 10 pillars are in three parts, four for the gate and three on each side, God's embrace of the world in the person of His Son, and fifteen cubits of fine linen on either side 3 × 5 (John 3:16). There are no cherubim in the embroidery of the gate, for He had come not to judge the world but to save (John 12:47).

The curtain of the gate was of needlework on fine linen, that is to say it was wrought on one side only. The thought conveyed by needlework is presentation of grace, whilst cunning work, that is both sides alike, is the representation of intrinsic excellence.

### The Brazen Altar

Exodus 27:1-8

The first thing that claims our attention on entering the Court of the Tabernacle is the brazen or copper Altar *(miz-bay-ack)*. This stood in the centre of the first square of the Court which measured 50 × 50 cubits. The term 'foursquare' indicates position as well as shape. This is indicated clearly by reference to the position of the altar in the vision of Ezekiel. "The court 100 cubits long, 100 cubits broad, foursquare and the altar that was before the house" (Ezekiel 40:47). In Ezekiel 48:20 the holy oblation is also foursquare, with the possession of the city, namely the city central. Also the heavenly Jerusalem is seen in the same relation in Revelation 21:16, "The city lieth foursquare." In the Tabernacle three things are spoken of as foursquare, the altar of burnt offering which we are considering (Exodus 27:1; 38:1); the breastplate on the heart of Aaron, indicating

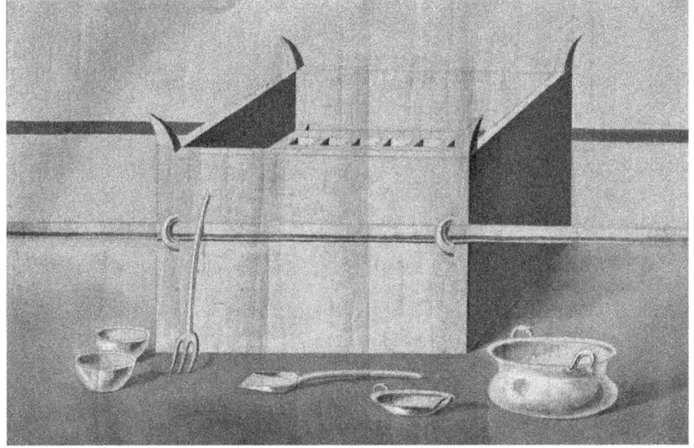

Figure 5: The Brazen Altar

the central place which belongs to Israel in the world to come (Exodus 28:16; 39:9); and the golden altar for incense which stood in the centre of the second square of 'The Holy' in the house (Exodus 30:2; 37:25), worship being the prime or central object.

The emphasis upon the central position for the vessel of sacrifice is important, for around the Cross of our Lord which it typifies, all the great truths of redemption gather.

In Ezekiel 43:15, the altar is called *'Har-el'* — the mountain of God. Isaiah 2:1 also alludes to this, "The mountain of the Lord's house shall be established in the top of the mountains." The Cross of Christ shall be pre-eminent in that day. Again in Ezekiel 43:16 it is called *'Ari-el'* — the lion of God, and our thoughts turn to the Lion of the tribe of Judah, the slain Lamb of Revelation 5:5-6, with its message of His supreme power and ability to accomplish the purpose of God. It was in the centre

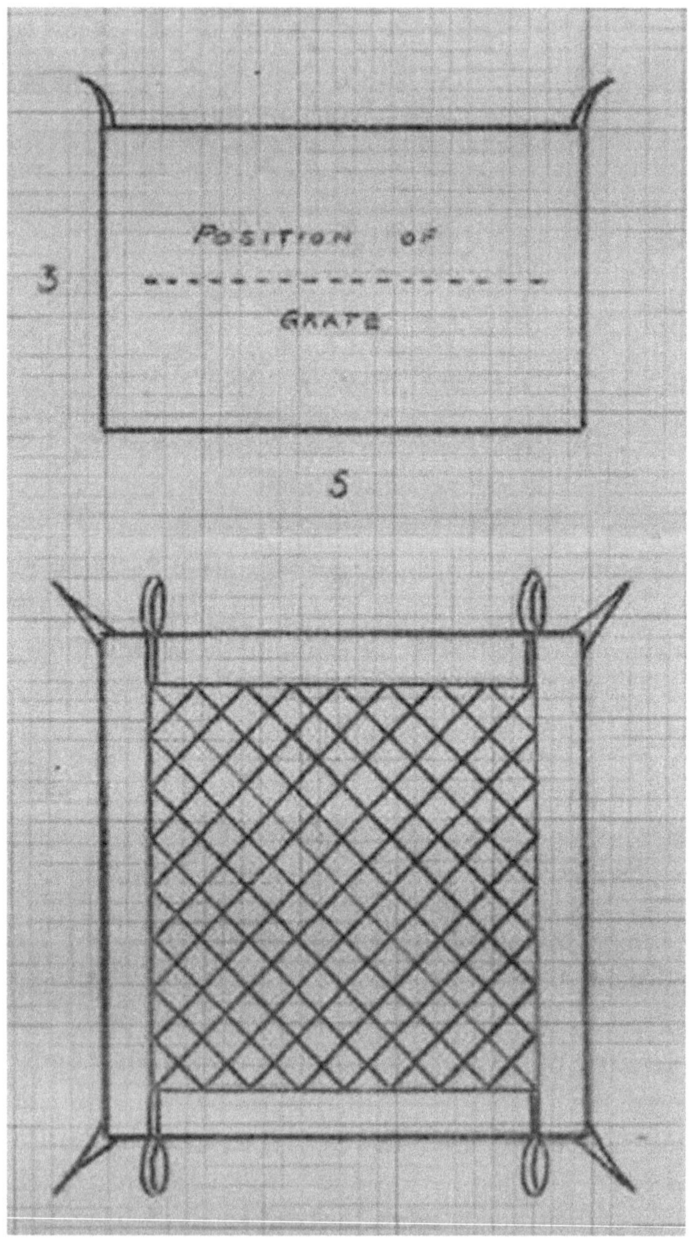


Figure 6: The Grate of the Brazen Altar

of the Court that Solomon's great sacrifice was offered (2.Chronicles 7:7).

F. W. Grant alluding to the altar (Ezekiel 40) says,

> "It was the actual centre of the whole sacred enclosure, at the centre of the inner court which measured 100 cubits each way. It is the Divine centre upon which every line of approach converges, east, north and south. It stands as the abiding memorial of Christ and His sacrifice. This is central to all blessing and glory in which Israel and the nations will participate, as indeed it is to the whole universe (Colossians 1:19-20). It will ever remind those who throng the courts of the Lord's house of the Lamb of God Who takes away the sin of the world. Upon the mount of transfiguration His death was the subject of converse. That scene set forth the glory of the Kingdom come in power, and when it is actually come, that death will not be forgotten. The peerless glory which will then invest Him, will not hide the truth of that redemption by blood upon which all action in power is based."[18]

"Thou shalt make an altar of acacia (shittim) wood." This was the timber tree of the desert, and it was in wilderness circumstances that the humanity of our Lord was displayed. The acacia, which the Septuagint renders 'incorruptible wood' because of its imperishable nature

18 F. W. Grant. *The Numerical Bible: Being a Revised Translation of the Holy Scriptures with Expository Notes: Arranged, Divided, and Briefly Characterized According to the Principles of their Numerical Structure*, Volume 4: Ezekiel. Neptune, NJ: Loizeaux Brothers, 1931.

and freedom from decay, is an apt symbol of the holy humanity in which Christ came in flesh. Though a man in very deed, yet His moral nature was an entirely new kind of humanity, seen in One Who did no sin, Who knew no sin, and in Whom was no sin, no act, no compromise possible. Nature refers to the inherent qualities of anything; the essential qualities which make it what it is in personal and characteristic quality. Therefore as relating to man as a race, human nature describes the quality or disposition, the humanity belonging to such. Our Lord did not belong to the race of Adam, and the qualities which characterised Him were of a far higher order. He was truly Man in spirit, soul and body, for of the latter it is said, "A body hast Thou prepared Me" {Hebrews 10:5}.This was formed in the womb of the Virgin by Divine power, but in all that pertained to moral being our Lord was not as the first man of the earth, earthy, but was from or out of heaven, deriving nothing from the nature of her of whom He was born, otherwise there would have been in Him the same possibility to sin as in the first Adam (compare 1 John 3:9). See J.N.D. *Synopsis* Volume 4, pages 269-270.

In size the Altar was five cubits long and five cubits broad, this representing that the work of redemption was accomplished by our Lord in man's capacity. In height it was three cubits, the sign of the Divine approval. Adding this three to the height five the number 8 is found, expressive of Divine power, to which the Resurrection bore witness. This is further borne out by the horns, equivalent of power, pointing upwards — ascension; and four in number for the witness of this is worldwide to all men. The dimensions of the Altar are the same as the brazen scaffold which Solomon made and on which he stood, and which no doubt signifies that all the glory of which he was a figure, and all blessing in answer to intercession rests upon the Altar of Sacrifice (2 Chronicles 6:13).

The tabernacle altar, 5 × 5 × 3, differs in dimension from the altar in Solomon's temple, 20 × 20 × 10 (2 Chronicles 4:1), and from Ezekiel's, 12 × 12 × 4; the first speaking of God's will borne witness to in public display, the second to Worldwide administration (Ezekiel 43:13-17).

The whole of the Altar was covered with copper, significant of One Who could sustain the righteousness of God in respect of sin and endure the fire of His holy judgment.

In construction it was hollow, and we may gather from Exodus 20:24 that it was partly filled with earth. In His death our Lord descended into the lowest parts of the earth. Thus the acacia wood covered with copper shows that Christ sustained in the place of death the holy requirements of God in respect of sin (John 10:17), infinitely acceptable to Him and by which He is glorified. The four brazen rings testify to the eternal result, for He "of God is made unto us wisdom, and righteousness, and sanctification, and redemption" {1 Corinthians 1:30}. But these rings were attached to the corners of a network or grate of copper which rested upon a ledge, as the word 'compass' implies in the midst of the altar. This is significant, for the death of Jesus was not merely that of a martyr, nor limited to outward sufferings of the body, but lay in the depths of His Soul's anguish as bearing sin. "When Thou shalt make His soul an offering for sin" {Isaiah 53:10}. It was this that brought from His holy lips the cry, "My God, My God, why hast Thou forsaken Me?" Through the rings, and they are the only four copper rings in the Tabernacle, the staves likewise of acacia wood and copper covered were passed when the altar was carried, symbolic of the gospel testimony which ever witnesses that Christ suffered for sins, the Just for the unjust to bring us to God {1 Peter 3:18}. No dimensions are given for the grate[19] of copper, for the work of the Cross cannot be measured, for it is infinite.

Later on, a covering of broad plates was made for the altar of the copper censers of those who were involved in the rebellion of Korah, prominence being thereby given to the certainty of judgment for any who despise the sacrifice on which approach to God is founded (Numbers 16:36-40).

The four sides of the Altar have each a special message. On the east side, that nearest to the gate, and which first met the eyes of those who entered, was a heap of ashes (Leviticus 1:16). This spoke of the sacrifice over, the work done; it told of acceptance, in the full value of what the altar stood for. On the north side the victim was slain, it was the place of death, as it shall be the place of manifested victory. "On the sides of the north, the city of the great King" {Psalm 48:2}. The north side is significant of Him Who laid down His life, no man taking it from Him. It may be that to give point to this the victim was not slain upon the altar as in heathen sacrifice, it was the dust which received the poured out blood. "Ye shall pour all the blood at the bottom of the

[19] The word for grate occurs only in this connection. It is derived from a word meaning 'to plait' and from the same root we have the word 'sieve' in Amos 9:9. {*mikbar*} 'grate'. {*karkob*} 'ledge round', so Revised Version, a word nowhere else used and whose derivation is not absolutely clear. It is said to be derived from a word meaning 'to surround' hence border or compass would be the proper rendering.

altar" (Leviticus 4:7). "Thou hast brought Me into the dust of death" (Psalm 22:15). It was at the north gate in the vision of Ezekiel that provision was made for the accomplishment of the work of sacrifice (Ezekiel 40:35-43), whether burnt offering, trespass offering or sin offering (Ezekiel 40:39). In Scripture the north is associated with judgment; it was from that quarter that the stroke fell upon Israel and Judah (Jeremiah 1:14). The word *'tzaphon'* — north — means that which is dark, hidden, and is used of the quarter that is ever associated with mystery and gloom. In presence of this we cannot fail to recall the darkness of Golgotha, and the mystery of the anguish of suffering into which the soul of our Saviour entered that the blackness of darkness for ever might not be our portion.

On the other hand, the south side was the place from which the waters flowed in the same vision of Ezekiel 47:1. It speaks of the blessing which is the result of sacrifice, and of the abundant fulness flowing from the heart of God. The west side towards the laver and the house was God's side, it spoke of the solution of the sin question to His glory, so that every Divine attribute is in perfect harmony in giving access into His presence. "Having therefore, brethren, boldness to enter into the holiest by the blood of Jesus" {Hebrews 10:19}. The west also speaks of the close of man's day, but holding in itself the promise of a morning without clouds in the light of Him Whose coming is as sure as the dawn.

The Tabernacle was but the shadow of good things to come and not the very image of the things, for no blood offered upon the Altar of the Court could ever take away sins. For this reason, no seats were provided in the Tabernacle, for the work of the priests was never finished, they could never sit down. "But this Man after

He had offered one sacrifice for sins, for ever sat down" {Hebrews 10:12}. Such is the witness of the Holy Spirit to the finished work of which the brazen altar was but a shadow.

The reference to the horns in Psalm 118:27, words which our Lord uttered in the Psalm He sung with His disciples ere leaving the upper chamber (John 14), remind us of His devotion unto death: "Bind the sacrifice with cords even to the horns of the altar".

The carrying of the vessels by means of the staves signifies the testimony borne in Levitical service to that which the vessels stood for. This is the witness of the saints to the truth of the Person and Work of Christ, and should be central in all ministry.[20]

Coverings were provided for the Altar and these also speak of witness to His excellence. The altar was completely covered with a purple cloth, over which was a covering of badger skins (Numbers 4). The purple speaks of the universal glorious reign of the Son of Man. It was only on the Altar that this colour was put, for the sufferings of Christ are most intimately connected with the glory that shall follow. He Who has worn the crown of thorns shall wear many crowns of glory and be acclaimed King of Kings and Lord of Lords. All this is hidden as yet, and the world sees only the badger skins, and sees no beauty beneath that they should desire Him.[21]

### Utensils

The utensils of the Altar were five in number.

20 Some suppose the altar to have been filled with earth, see Exodus 20:24, and that for this purpose the shovels were provided.

21 There was no bottom to the altar, indicating infinitude.

*Ash-pans* or pots (*'siroth'*) from a word meaning 'to boil'; they were the witness of the accomplished sacrifice. Two Hebrew words are used for ashes. One is the general term largely used in the language of mourning. The other is only used in connection with the sacrifices and literally means 'fat'.[22] It has been thought that this is because of the burning of the fat upon the altar which would saturate the ashes. Ashes are evidence that the sacrifice was accomplished and accepted. The {Authorized Version} marginal reference to Psalm 20:3, "The Lord turn to *ashes* thy burnt sacrifice", says 'make fat'.

*Shovels.* (*'gah')* from a root meaning 'to snatch' or 'sweep away'. The witness of that which is over, completed, finished.

*Basons.* (*'mizrekoth'*) from a root meaning 'to sprinkle'. The blood was first offered — the fact of death having taken place; it was then sprinkled — the application for purification.

*Flesh-hooks.* (*'mizlegoth'*) from a root meaning to 'draw up'. Every part of the sacrifice was laid in order, there was no chance occurrence in our Lord's offering, all was foreseen.

*Fire-pans.* (*'makathoth'*) from a root meaning 'to take up fire'. The same word is used for snuff-dishes and censers.

---

22 {*dashen*} 'shall be made fat' (Proverbs 11:25, 13:4, 28:25; Isaiah 34:6-7).
{*deshen*} 'fatness' (Judges 9:9; Job 36:16; Isaiah 55:2; Jeremiah 31:14).
{*deshen*} 'ashes' (Leviticus 1:16, 4:12; 6:10-11; 1 Kings 13:3, 5; Jeremiah 31:40).
{*eper*} 'ashes' . . . . . . . . mourning {Isaiah 61:2-3}; of the red heifer {Numbers 19:9-10, 17}
{*apar*} 'ashes' . . . . . . . usually 'dust', as Genesis 2:7.
{*piyah*} 'ashes' . . . . . . of furnace (Exodus 9:8, 10).

Fire was carried from the altar to light the incense, any other would have been strange fire. Worship must always be connected with the sacrifice. Sacrifice alone can accomplish the restitution of the moral order and establish righteousness. This is seen in the first case in a man who came into right relationship with God by blood-shedding, the best fruits of Creation being no substitute for this. This is a fundamental principle which abides for all time and underlies all approach to God. It was the gift that Abel brought, not that which his labour had produced, as Cain. It may be that God had given a basis for Abel's faith in the death of the animals whose skins formed the clothing of Adam and Eve. The fig leaves were sewed by themselves and were inadequate to cover the nakedness, the consciousness of which bore witness that they were sinners. The coats of skins were God provided and God wrought: 'God shall provide Himself a lamb'.

### Purpose

In use the Altar was for burnt-offering, it represented acceptance in the value of the sacrifice offered, at the same time the blood of the sin-offering was put upon its horns. Various indeed are the aspects of the death of our Lord, but the offering is one.

The Altar had thus a twofold purpose — to offer the burnt offering and to bear witness to the sprinkled blood. In the first full acceptance was declared and in the second, expiation. Ahaz put the Brazen Altar to one side and substituted a human and heathen device. He also lowered the sea, which took the place of the Laver in the Tabernacle, to the level of a pavement of stones {2 Kings 16:15-17}. This was equivalent to setting aside the cross of Christ and lowering the word of God to the

### Blood in the New Testament

Blood of the new covenant (testament) – Matthew 26:28, Mark 14:24.

Blood of the new covenant – Luke 22:20, 1 Corinthians 11:25.

Blood of sprinkling – Hebrews 12:24.

Blood of Jesus – Hebrews 10:19.

Blood of Christ – 1 Corinthians 10:16, Ephesians 2:13, 1 Peter 1:19, Hebrews 9:14.

Blood of Jesus Christ – 1 Peter 1:2.

Blood of His Son – 1 John 1:7.

Blood of the Lamb – Revelation 7:14, 12:11.

Blood of the Lord – 1 Corinthians 11:27.

Blood of remission – Hebrews 9:22.

Blood of dedication – Hebrews 9:11{-12}.

Blood of everlasting covenant – Hebrews 13:20.

Blood of covenant (old) – Hebrews 9:20.

Blood of His cross – Colossians 1:20.

Blood of His own – Acts 20:28, Hebrews 9:12.

Blood of redemption – Ephesians 1:7, Colossians 1:14, Revelation 5:9.

Blood of peace – Colossians 1:20.

Blood of sanctification – Hebrews 10:29, 13:12.

Blood of justification – Romans 5:9.

Blood of righteousness – Romans 3:25.

Blood of life – John 6:54-56.

Blood of purchase – Acts 20:28.

Blood of communion (fellowship) – 1 Corinthians 10:16.

Blood of freedom (loosed) – Revelation 1:5.

level of mere human literature. There is no cleansing power in stones, nor acceptance on other altars.

### Numerical Symbolism

The following note on the altar in the temple of Ezekiel will show the numerical symbolism.

> "Ezekiel's altar is 12 × 12 cubits; 2 cubits higher than that in the first temple and 8 cubits less in length and breadth.
>
> Its principal dimensions are 18, 16, 14, 12 cubits. The common divisor of these numbers is 2 = competent witness and fellowship. Dividing the numbers by this we obtain 9, 8, 7, 6. Thus we have the complete idea of fullest manifestation, (9 = 3 × 3), in the power of the Spirit and the glory of resurrection (3); and this in new covenant relation (8) into which all creation (4) will then be brought according to perfection and rest (7), crowned of necessity with mastery over evil by the work of Christ (6).
>
> The topmost part, of the structure is foursquare, 12 cubits on each side, (4 × 3), the number of Divine government exercised throughout creation according to the fulness of Godhead dwelling in Christ; to which fulness all things in heaven and on earth are reconciled in the power of the blood of the Cross, by which peace has been made.
>
> {...When the redeemed creation will be enjoying the accomplishment of all that we now know to be God's purpose and which gives cause for present rejoicing in the Lord,

we shall be with Him, sharing as the Body with the Head in all the various features of that glorious kingdom, not in an earthly but heavenly relation. And though we shall then be in the glory and around the throne forever, we will never fail to look at and consider the place of sacrifice, viewing it then from the inner Sanctuary.} The Lamb shall be seen in the midst of the throne" (F. W. Grant).[23]

## The Laver

The next vessel of the Court to claim our attention is the Laver and its foot. This stood between the Altar and the Tabernacle itself. It was composed entirely of copper, no size, no weight or dimension being specified for it. It had no covering, neither was any means of carrying it provided. These omissions would indicate that it represents that which cannot be fully known. The words "A statute for ever to them" {Exodus 30:21} show that it expresses something that is eternal, and at the same time that its use was to be continual. Along with the incense altar it is not mentioned until the priestly vestments of Aaron and his sons have been specified. Both these vessels are for priestly use. The Laver speaks of the death of Christ in its continual application, not in the aspect of blood but of water. In water the idea conveyed is removal, for water is a figure not only of death, circumcision was that, but of burial, baptism being the symbol of this. The Altar and the Laver give the whole import of the Cross. The first is expiation once for all, the latter is the entire putting off of the flesh

23 F. W. Grant. *The Numerical Bible: Being a Revised Translation of the Holy Scriptures with Expository Notes: Arranged, Divided, and Briefly Characterized According to the Principles of their Numerical Structure, Volume 4: Ezekiel.* Neptune, NJ: Loizeaux Brothers, 1931.

Figure 7: The Laver

once for all. It is this that has to be had in constant remembrance in all approach to God.

"Always bearing about in the body the dying of Jesus, that the life also of Jesus may be manifest in our mortal flesh." In that life the priestly family of God live, in that they draw near to offer the sacrifice of praise and worship, and to do this now that the reality has superceded the shadow in the Holiest of all. In Hebrews 10 the Altar and Laver are brought together, "Your hearts sprinkled from an evil conscience" — (blood) — "and your bodies washed with pure water". Both are needed if entrance into the sanctuary is to be known. It is said, "That they die not" {Exodus 30:21}. "If we would judge ourselves we should not be judged" (1 Corinthians 11:31). When water stands alone it is the Word of God for this is the means of cleansing and application. In connection with the copper its immediate reference is to death. When “living” or “running” is connected with water it represents the Holy Spirit. When water precedes the mention of blood as in the case of Aaron and his sons (Exodus 29:4), it stands for new birth. When water follows the mention of blood it refers to removal or cleansing by means of death, this may be either positional or practical as in the use of the Laver.

The copper, which signifies God’s unyielding character in judgment and in testing all things by His holiness, was obtained from the brazen mirrors of the women assembling at the door of the Court. The mirror speaks of the vanity and self-occupation which begets pride (compare Isaiah 3:23). But in the Laver that which had been the reflection of human fairness was under the water and this in turn became a mirror to reflect the face of heaven. God’s grace alone can convert a mirror of vanity into a laver of cleansing.

The bases in Solomon’s temple answer to the foot of the laver, the word being derived from the same root, and the sea that he made seems to have replaced the Laver, whilst the 10 lavers which he made were used for the washing of such things as belonged to the burnt offering (2 Chronicles 4:6).

The Laver is only mentioned once after the account of its construction, when it was anointed by Moses (Leviticus 8:11).

## Chapter 16: The Tabernacle or House

This will be our next consideration. Its total length was 30 cubits and its breadth 10 cubits.[24] It consisted of two chambers, the first or 'Holy' measuring 20 cubits long by 10 cubits wide, the second or 'Holiest' being a cube 10 × 10 × 10 cubits.

These two chambers were separated from each other by a hanging called "The Vail", whilst the whole was distinguished from the Court by another hanging called "The Door". In Hebrews 9:1-8 these are called the first and second veils, and the chambers are called the first and second tabernacles. The significance of this is that the separation showed that under the law the way into the Holiest of all was not open.

Comparing the dimensions of Solomon's temple in 1 Kings 6, there is found greater length, breadth and height. The total length was 60 cubits, breadth 20 cubits,

24 Josephus speaking of the tabernacle says, "Its length when it was set up was 30 cubits and its breadth 10 cubits." This would appear to be the outside measure, for the 6 western boards would measure 9 cubits and assuming that the north and south sides overlapped thus, and that the boards were half a cubit thick this would give 10 cubits. (The thickness of the boards was not given.)

height 30 cubits, and while the proportion between the two parts was the same 40:20 the Holiest itself was a cube 20 × 20 × 20 cubits. Besides this a porch was added the same size as "The Holy" of the tabernacle 20 × 10.

In Ezekiel's temple the size of the Holy and Holiest are the same as in Solomon's. We have before noticed that when a number is squared it implies testimony, and when it is cubed it signifies certainty, that to which not only the word but the oath of God is attached. So the dimensions of the Holiest would attest the fact of every responsibility being met, and the fulfilment of the will of God borne witness to. The doubling of the number in the later temples adds the thought of the Divine witness displayed. At the same time it must be observed that the factors of all these numbers are 2, 3, 5 not 7, for they express God's witness to Himself in human conditions and not the fulness of the Divine purpose which eternity will reveal.

The Tabernacle was a foreshadowing of the Person and work of Christ, and hence the reality having now come, its detail can be read in the light of this. Solomon's temple is a figure of the millennial glory and will be better understood when that time shall come. Ezekiel's temple which will then be built (Zechariah 6:13), will be a symbol of eternal conditions. The house of the forest of Lebanon may represent the nations of the millennial day (compare Isaiah 60:12-13).[25]

25 The house of the forest of Lebanon 100 × 50, in height 30, having a porch measuring 50 × 30.

Figure 8: Board with tenons and Sockets of silver

## THE FOUNDATION

The foundation of the Tabernacle consisted of 100 sockets of silver, 96 of which supported the 48 boards of the house and 4 under the 4 pillars of the vail.[26]

Each of these sockets weighed a talent = 117 pounds Troy and there were two under each board. This metal was obtained from the money paid by each Israelite as the price of his redemption. Hence the symbol of silver is easily read, and the solid weight indicates the strong foundation which has been established by our Lord, not with corruptible silver but with His own precious blood. It is upon the work of the Cross that all things stand secure to the glory of God. See Exodus 38:25-28 for the total amount of silver in the Tabernacle and how it was used.

26 There were 2 sockets under each board which had two tenons, which may represent the twin principles of love and obedience by which our Lord accomplished the work the Father had given Him to do (John 14:31).

## THE WALLS

The sides of the Tabernacle consisted of boards, 20 on the north side, 20 on the south and 6 on the west, with 2 corner boards added, making 48 in all. This number may be read either as 4 × 12, representative of world-wide administration, or 6 × 8, work which is attested by power. The reign of our Lord Jesus Christ will answer to both. It is of Him that the boards speak, being made of the same acacia wood as the altar. The expression as to the boards 'standing up' indicates their connection with the truth which reaches to Christ in glory. In length they measured 10 cubits and in breadth 1½ cubits. The half or cut cubit reminds us of the cutting off of Messiah (Daniel 9:26), upon which fact the new administration is established, every responsibility Godward having been met (10). The same thought seems to be emphasised in the two corner boards, for these were cut lengthwise and joined or as in the {Authorized Version} margin, twinned, as a joiner would join them at a right angle so as to embrace the junction of the sides.[27]

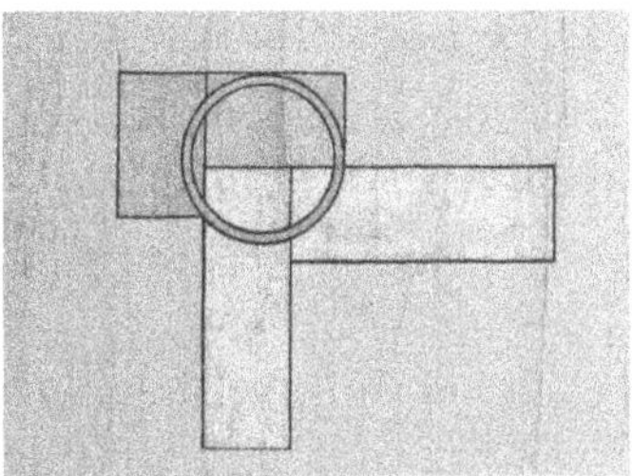

Figure 9: Arrangement of the corner Boards

27 "Then I apprehend not as once I thought, that the corners were doubled to strengthen them, not cut off so as to destroy the square inside, and make it 10 cubits wide, or more; but thus the six boards giving the breadth unchanged" (*Notes and Comments*, J.N.Darby, Volume I, page 320).

These corner boards speak of Him Who holds all together in security by the power of His redemption,[28] the silver sockets at the base, His person and work, and at the top, at the head, by a ring of gold.[29]

The rings are attached to the boards, indicating the response of love in man to Divine love, perfectly seen in Christ. The separate ring as in the corner board is expressive of God's love.

We shall meet with many rings in the Tabernacle, all with the same meaning, love and union, a thought which we always associate with a wedding ring. How precious it is to remember that all is secure both in righteousness laid in the lowest place and love established in the highest. The two boards are the witness of this. Each board had fixed in it three rings of gold, the Divine expression of love, and through these rings bars of the same material were passed. These clearly indicate power. There were five on each side reminding us that it is in the Man Christ Jesus that love and power combine. The middle bar passed from end to end, not through the substance of the bars as some have thought, but through the rings which are said to be places for the bars. The remaining four bars extended only half way. This again would seem to indicate that whilst the purpose of God stands unchanged, as seen in the three centre bars, the 12 divided ones would point to a postponement of the time when the government shall be upon the shoulder of Messiah the King, occasioned by His rejection. This division has to be observed in reading the prophets who speak of His coming glory.

28 The cutting and joining may indicate, "I lay down my life that I may take it again" {John 10:17}.

29 *'Tabba'ath'* = 'ring' is properly 'a seal', i.e. a signet and hence a ring of any kind.

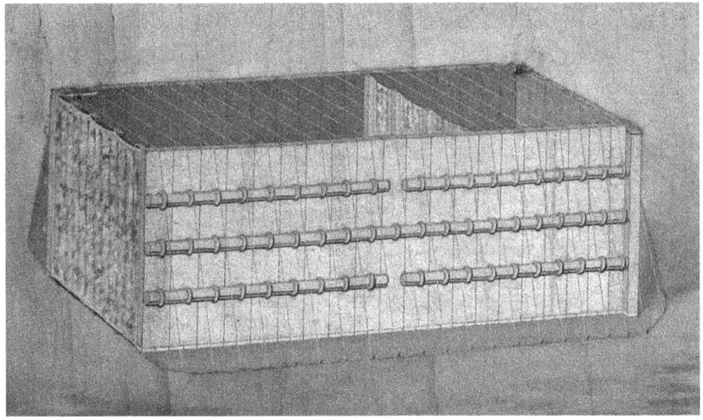

Figure 10: The Door and the Vail, with the bars and boards of the Walls

Five pillars of acacia wood and gold supported the hanging which formed the door of the Tabernacle. These had sockets of copper, with capitals and connecting rods (fillets) of gold and hooks of gold. All this speaks of a glorified Christ, such as is presented in the epistles of the New Testament. The pillars may remind us that the Holy Spirit used five writers for these, Paul, Peter, James, John and Jude. The teaching of these epistles concerns Christ crowned with glory and honour, the golden capitals; and that all things depend on Him, golden hooks. At the same time all is founded in Divine righteousness, to which the Roman epistle bears witness, copper sockets.

Viewing the boards as typical of a privileged people we are "all one in Christ Jesus" {Galatians 3:28} There were 48 boards, and the Apostle Paul in his letters uses the words "in Christ Jesus" 48 times {J.N.D. translation}.

In this aspect the bars may well represent the practical means which God has provided in order that the saints might be preserved in unity:

| | |
|---|---|
| Ephesians 4{:2-3} | 1. Lowliness; 2. Meekness;<br>3. Longsuffering; 4. Forbearance;<br>5. Endeavouring to keep the unity of the Spirit in the uniting bond of peace (The centre bar.) |

Or again, the gifts:

| | |
|---|---|
| {Ephesians 4:11} | 1. Apostles. 2. Prophets.<br>3. Evangelists. 4. Pastors.<br>5. Teachers. |
| Colossians 3:12 | 1. Mercies. 2. Kindness.<br>3. Humbless. 4. Meekness.<br>5. Longsuffering. |

The personal titles of Christ may be seen in groups of five:

| | |
|---|---|
| Isaiah 9:6 | 1. Wonderful; 2. Counsellor;<br>3. The Mighty God;<br>4. The Everlasting Father;<br>5. The Prince of Peace. |
| Colossians 1:15-17 | 1. Image of the invisible God;<br>2. Firstborn; 3. Creator ("by Him");<br>4. Object ("for Him"); 5. Upholder. |
| Hebrews 1:2-3 | 1. Heir; 2. Creator;<br>3. Brightness of manifestation;<br>4. Express image; 5. Upholder. |

The vail which shut in the Holiest was suspended upon four pillars, likewise of acacia wood and gold, but socketed in silver. In this case although there were hooks of gold there were no capitals, for the vail is

Figure 11: Cut-away view of the Pillars and Vail

typical of Christ's flesh, and in this He suffered with no crown but one of thorns. Thus the four writers of the Gospels present Him to us, at the same time they show the redemption work accomplished, the ransom paid, the silver sockets. It will be noticed how the glory of His person is maintained throughout, in the gold and wood which formed the solid support for the fabrics which typified His mediatorial glories. These are displayed in the curtains, the tent, coverings, hanging for the door, and the vail.

The gold is not mentioned until *all* the boards and bars have been described; unity is the thought in this, for as seen in Christ, the Divine testimony was marked by unity of purpose.

Cords and pins were provided as in the pillars of the court. In relation to the boards, the cords would appear to have passed over the top from side to side. Security was obtained in every detail connected with the wilderness.

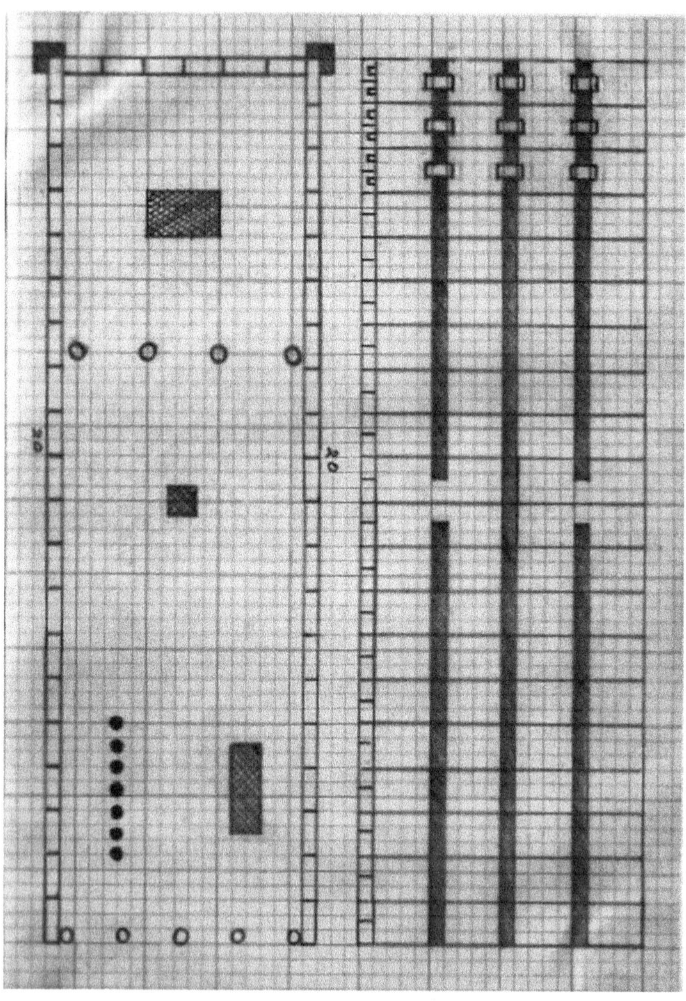


Figure 12: Plan and elevation views of the layout of the pillars, boards and bars of the Walls

## The Embroidered Curtains

Ten curtains of fine twined linen and blue and purple and scarlet, embroidered in which were cherubims, formed the tabernacle properly so called — 'One Tabernacle' (Exodus 26:6). (The curtains are called 'The Tabernacle' in Exodus 26:1, 6; 36:8, 13; Numbers 3:25.) The whole was of cunning work, that is both sides alike, not wrought upon the surface of one side which was the case when needlework was specified. Each curtain measured 28 cubits in length and 4 cubits in breadth, in which the factors 7 and 4 are apparent, speaking of perfection manifest in Christ on earth. The foundation fabric was of fine twined linen, which, like the curtains forming the court, expressed the holy righteousness of the life of our Lord. The total length of the curtains, 280 cubits, corresponded to the length of the white linen curtains of the court, omitting the hanging of the gate, 280 cubits. The white, blue, purple and scarlet express the four characters of Sonship pertaining to Christ.

### White

He is the Son of God's love; He was ever such in the eternal ages; He was such here on earth: upon Him the Father opened the heavens to exclaim, "Thou art My beloved Son, in whom is all My delight."

### Blue

He is the Son of God come from heaven, the revealer of the Father, the second person of the Trinity, God manifest in flesh, Image of the Invisible in man's lowly guise. But what has He revealed? The fountain of Divine Love has poured forth its fulness in Him, and this must not be forgotten in the symbol of the blue.

### Purple

The imperial colour speaks of the universal supremacy of the Son of Man into Whose hands the Father has committed all things, and given Him authority to execute judgment also because He is the Son of Man. This explains also the meaning of the cherubim woven in the curtains, for these represent the execution of the judgment of God according to the attributes of His holy nature. The presence of the cherubim in curtains and vail remind us of the Cross where Christ sustained the cherubic judgment of God against sin, and therefore all right of judgment is committed to Him, because He so suffered as Son of Man (John 5:27). We shall find them again in the vail and upon the ark, but not in the hanging of the door or the gate of the court for these present the grace of God inviting both the sinner and the saint to draw near.

### Scarlet

— has a double significance. It is Israel's royal colour and hence marks out our Lord Jesus Christ as Son of David. He is the rod out of the stem of Jesse, and the Branch out of his roots. Scarlet speaks also of consecration unto death involving redemption for those whose sins were as scarlet and crimson in the sight of God. The curtains as a whole set forth the glories of Christ as Mediator, for only the Son become man could be this, in order that He might reconcile all things to God, first by the death of the Cross and then by a dominating power which will subdue all things unto Himself in order that the Triune God may be all in all. Then shall things be brought into harmony with God. His nature at last shall hold absolute sway in the universe, and this shall be by the mediatorial,

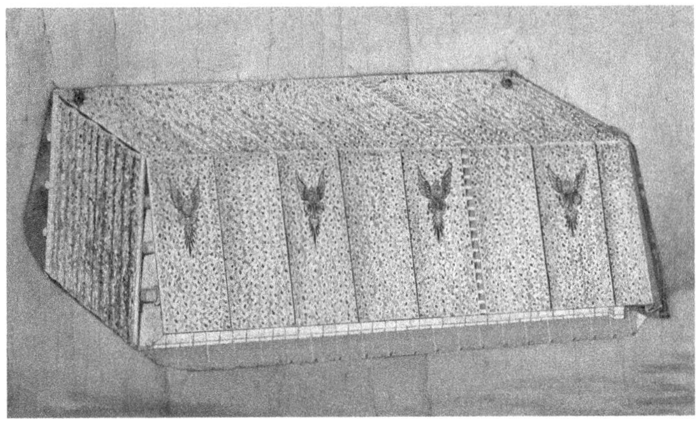

Figure 13: The Embroidered Curtains

redeeming, reconciling, recreating work of the Son. Such is the lesson of the curtains, no wonder that the epistle to the Hebrews speaks of the Tabernacle as the shadow of good things to come.

There is more yet to learn, for these ten curtains were joined together in two sets of five, these sets being coupled together by fifty golden taches in loops of blue upon the selvedge. Ten naturally reminds us of the ten commandments, five of which were Godward and five manward. It is the number of responsibility, and this seen perfectly in Christ, in His life on earth. The law was magnified and made honourable, and that in perfect adjustment of the claims of God and in relation to men. Fifty taches of gold, 10 × 5, harmonise with the number of the curtains, and loops of blue, for only a Divine person could accomplish, in grace and love, this harmony. The vail hung immediately under the taches, giving added emphasis to His humanity Who took upon Him the form of a servant.

Divine righteousness has met every demand. Christ has coupled in one great obedience man's fullest responsibility on both the Divine and human side. In Him was fully expressed love to God and love to man. The curtains are spoken of as 'one tabernacle'. In Hebrews 9:2-3, apparently they were regarded as forming two, but it is the vail being rent which explains the secret of the type. The four colours of the curtains are seen also in the Gospels:

| | | |
|---|---|---|
| Blue | Son of God | John |
| Scarlet | Son of David | Mark |
| White | Son of God's love | Luke |
| Purple | Son of Man | Matthew[30] |

In Matthew's Gospel, Christ lays aside His glory as Son of David to take up the wider glory of Son of Man, hence the need of Mark's Gospel to emphasise David's Son as the Servant (compare Isaiah 49:1-12).

The colours are not always referred to in the same order; in the curtains we have been considering, the white fine linen is put first, as it is also in the inner girdle of the high priest; in the ephod, gold is first; in the vail, door, and gate the blue is first. The emphasis being in each case upon the first colour mentioned.

It has been noticed that the colours are really purple blue, purple red and crimson, so that through all there was pervading a tinge of blue, the heavenly colour.

The curtains also reveal Christ as Mediator of the New Covenant. As Son of David He is the One by Whom the Word of God will be fulfilled. As Son of Man He will accomplish all the will of God. As Son of God He will make effectual the knowledge of God. As son of God's

30 The title 'Son of Man' occurs in Matthew 31 times, in Luke 25 times, in Mark 15 times and in John 12 times.

love He will establish the grace of God in the universe, compare Hebrews 8:10-12 for the four provisions of the New Covenant: (1) Divine writing; (2) Divine relationship; (3) Divine knowledge; (4) Divine forgiveness.

The fine twined linen or byssus, ('silk' as Genesis 41:42 {Authorized Version} margin; J.N.Darby gives 'fine Egyptian cotton'; Septuagint *βυσσον*; Hebrew *'shesh'*) represents the personal purity of Christ. His life was one complete whole; acts, words, attributes, character, details of life, facts and principles were inseparably and harmoniously blended, twined and wrought into one whole.

## The Tent

Over the curtains, or Tabernacle, there was a Tent consisting of eleven curtains of goats' hair, literally 'goats', the fabric being wrought by the labour of the women, as in the case of the curtains (Exodus 35:25-26). Each curtain measured 30 cubits in length, by 4 in width, the numbers being significant of responsibility divinely met, 10 × 3 = 30, by a work done in man's condition, 6 × 5 = 30. The four cubits embodies the thought of "Christ the Saviour of the world" (John 4:42). Six of the curtains were joined together, and five were also joined, and the two sets were coupled with 50 taches of copper. The mention of goats and copper instinctively lead to the thought of the Altar and the goat of the sin offering, and the fact that the Tent when joined covered all beneath it, has the typical teaching of 'atonement', an Old Testament word which means 'to cover'. Eleven is the number of the sin offering, rightly coming between the ten of responsibility and the twelve of administrative blessing. It is significant that 'one kid

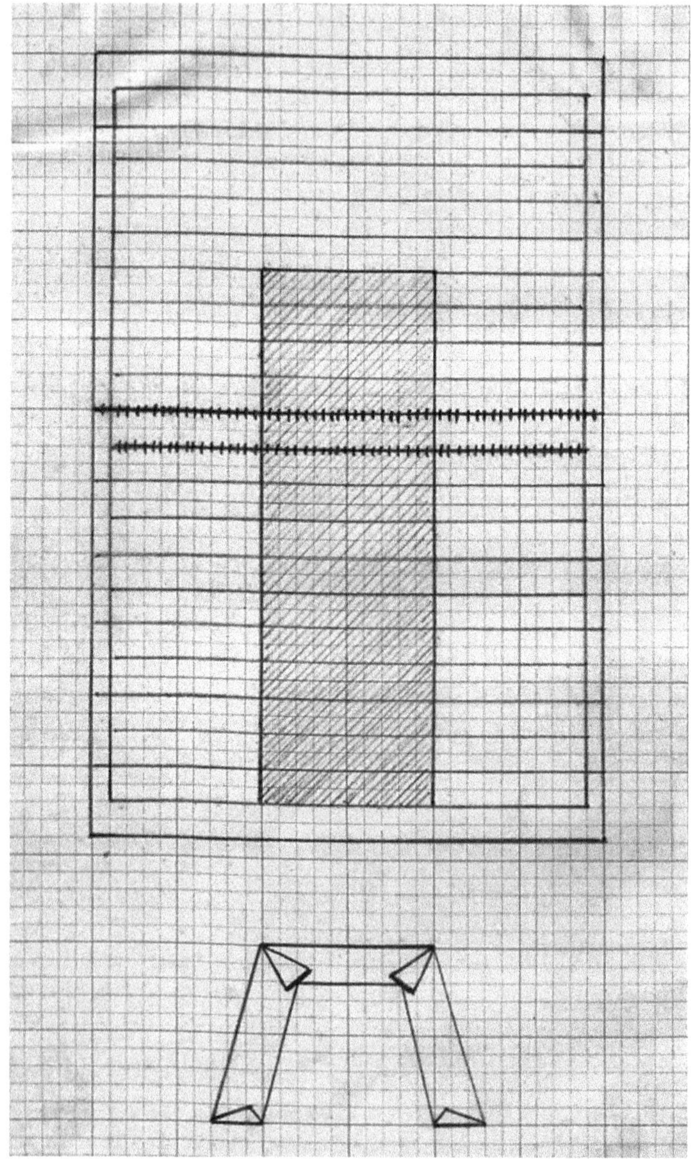

Figure 14: Eleven goats' hair curtains of the Tent covering the ten embroidered curtains of the Tabernacle

of the goats for a sin offering' was selected on eleven different occasions and no more.

| | | |
|---|---|---|
| 1. | Sin offering | Leviticus 4:23, 28. |
| 2. | Trespass offering | Leviticus 5:6. |
| 3. | Feast of Unleavened bread | Numbers 28:{22}. |
| 4. | Feast of Pentecost | Leviticus 23:19; Numbers 28:30. |
| 5. | Feast of Trumpets | Numbers 29:5. |
| 6. | Day of Atonement | Numbers 29:11. |

These six had their aspect towards man and may be represented by the six curtains joined by themselves.

| | | |
|---|---|---|
| 7. | New Moon | Numbers 28:15. |
| 8. | Ignorance offering of the congregation | Numbers 15:24. |
| 9. | Consecration of priests | Leviticus 9:3. |
| 10. | Dedication of the altar | Numbers 7:16. |
| 11. | Feast of Tabernacles | Numbers 29:16. |

These five had their aspect Godward, and may be represented by the five curtains joined together and which covered the Holiest.

The 50 clasps of copper suggest the thought of the altar which alone could bring God and man together. "There is one Mediator between God and man, the Man Christ Jesus." The clasps of copper did not coincide with the golden clasps which were over the vail, but were distant from these, half a curtain over the Holiest. This perhaps indicates that the Mediator was provided from God's side. It was God Who gave His Son.

Figure 15: The Tent of goats' hair

The type of the goat did not go so far as that of the lamb, the goat being the animal of atonement and the lamb of reconciliation. The first covered sin, the second removed it. Hence atonement is not spoken of in the New Testament, but Christ is seen as the Lamb of God, the taker away of sin by the sacrifice of Himself.

When placed in position, the Tent completely covered the Tabernacle, with a half curtain doubled in front, and a half curtain hanging down at the back. The doubling in front was a witness to all men who drew near, that approach to God was not on the ground of works but of atonement. The doubled curtain hung over the door in token of acceptance. The work however that secured this, (note that it was the sixth curtain that was doubled) was also sufficient to meet the claims and glory of God and maintain the holiness of His throne. Of this the half curtain at the back bore testimony.

There is another thought connected with goats' hair, which is not disconnected with the foregoing. It points to the positive purity of Christ, the severity of evil which surrounded Him from which He was entirely separate, which gave Him the character of Prophet. His severity of separation was not towards sinners but apart from them, as in Psalm 1:1. He wore the moral garment of hair which distinguished the prophet (Zechariah 13:4; Matthew 3:4). For us, this is the bearing in our body the dying of Jesus, the separating power of the Cross of the Sin-bearer from the sin which He bore in His own body on the tree.

## The Coverings

### The rams' skins

These were two coverings. The first of rams' skins dyed red, the second of badger or seal skins. No measure was specified for these, an indication that they typified that which was entirely for God and was without limit. The rams' skins speak of consecration, the badger skins of separation. The ram was the consecration offering and it represents Christ in the energy of purpose which devoted Himself even to death. The skins suggest this character which marked His life, and that they were dyed red shows how intense and real this character was, in its intensity and devotion to the will of God and His glory which found its full expression in the death of the Cross. F. W. Grant in *'Leaves from the Book'* page 260, remarks, "The ram is not simply the sheep, the meek surrenderer of life, but as being the male sheep, imports the bringing into this surrender a firmer and stronger will, an energy of character which makes it purposeful, determinate surrender."

Red or scarlet brings before us the thought of devotion, but it was also Israel's royal colour, and there is a connection between these two ideas, for it was in the laying aside of His royal rights as King, that His devotion to God is seen, which was expressed in His

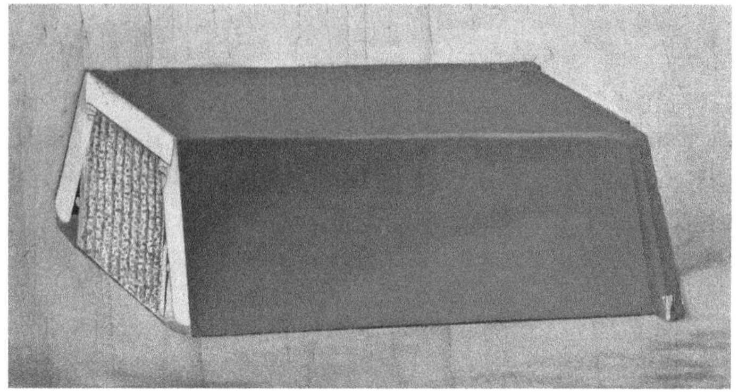

Figure 16: The covering of rams' skins

path of humiliation. The word used for 'dyed red' is '*dam*' signifying 'bloods' (*meoddammim*), and might be rendered 'rams' skins blood colour', putting a peculiar emphasis upon the type. It is a different word from that used for 'scarlet' in the curtains, vail, etc., which is '*tolath*' more properly 'warm colour' because of its origin from the insect 'coccus ilicis', the Septuagint rendering the word 'scarlet' by '*kokkivos*' and using a different word in the case of the rams' skins, *ἠρυθροδανωμένα* = 'dyed red'.

### Consecration

In speaking of the *consecration* of our Lord it is well to call to mind the four aspects of this subject presented in the Old Testament. In the {Authorized Version} New Testament the word 'consecrate' occurs but twice, in Hebrews 10:20, where *ἐνεκαίνισεν* would be better rendered 'he dedicated' and in Hebrews 7:28 where *τελειόω {τετελειωμένον}* is more accurately translated in the Revised Version 'perfected'. In the New Testament in place of 'consecrate' we have the words 'sanctify' and 'sanctification', and cognate with these the name of 'saints', or 'set apart ones', all of which shows how much greater is the substance in the New Testament than its shadow in the Old. Consecration has been defined as 'The act or ceremony of separating from a common to a sacred use, or devoting and dedicating a person or thing to the service or worship of God'.

There are four words in the Old Testament rendered 'consecrate' having reference to this as ceremonial or passive, voluntary or active, the consequent state or condition, and the objective result.

The first word is '*kadash*' meaning 'to set apart' or 'make holy' (Exodus 30:30). This was ceremonial as in the case of Aaron and his sons. It was what God did for them. He appointed them by the act to be priests that they might minister unto Him (Exodus 29:3-4, 41{,44}). It was their call, their setting apart, their consecration. Done once for all it was never renewed, it was done for them and continued for life.

The second word is '*nazar*' familiar to us in connection with the Nazarite vow (Numbers 6:12). Its meaning is 'to separate' and it is frequently so translated. It has also by implication the sense of 'a crown' in allusion to the unshorn head of the Nazarite, and is so translated in Exodus 29:6, Psalm 89:39 and Zechariah 9:16. '*Nazar*' has in it the thought of voluntary dedication either on the part of the person, or if from birth, of his parents, these latter having from the first to observe the Nazarite requirements (Judges 13:4-5). It was something done by the person or another on his behalf.

The third word is '*charam*' the meaning of which is 'to shut up', and it refers to a state of entire devotion to God and could never be recalled, it was irrevocable until death (Leviticus 27:28-29). The sentence 'It shall surely be put to death' apparently signifying that the living thing so devoted should remain in that state until death. The vow of *'charam'* was the most inexorable of Hebrew vows.

The fourth word is *'mala yad'* and means 'to fill the hand', signifying that the actual service of the life was to be for God, with no room for anything else {Exodus 32.29}.

Viewing consecration in the light afforded by these words we may see how perfectly our Lord answered to the type of the ram's skin dyed blood colour. He was *'kadash'* — God's set apart, holy One. He was the sent one of the Father, the One Whom the Father had sanctified and sent into the world. His mission was by Divine appointment and Divine endowment. He was consecrated by Eternal decree, by holy incarnation, and the definite public witness of the heavens concerning Him. The descent of the Holy Spirit at His baptism was His inauguration into His Messianic office.

Again, He was *'nazar'* by His voluntary act of self-dedication both in will and deed. 'I delight to do Thy will O My God' and this was so from His birth (Psalm 22:9-10; Isaiah 49:1-3). Rejected as the sent One of the Father, the blessing of Israel is postponed, and our Lord becomes *'nazar'* in another sense. He has taken upon Himself the Nazarite vow during this term of His being separate from earthly joy with His people Israel. He drinks no more of the fruit of the vine until the Kingdom of God shall come (Matthew 26:29). This sanctifying or setting apart is in view of heavenly purposes, that through His Cross, resurrection and ascension to glory, His Own might in separation from the world share His victory and have part with Him in the joy of the Father's presence.

The consecration of our Lord was also 'charam': He entered this world that He might die. No offer of the world's glory could turn Him from this purpose and with steadfast heart He set His face towards the Cross as the end of His pathway here below. The inexorable claims of this vow may be seen in Philippians 2:7-8 and in Hebrews 2:9.

Then how truly was He *'mala yad'*, His hands filled with service for God and man. He had indeed come not to be ministered unto but to minister, and amongst His Own He was as one that serveth. None of the objects that engrossed the minds of men occupied His thoughts or distracted Him from this service. His hands were full of grace and truth and He dispensed the goodness of God in every place abundantly.

All sanctification is derived from the holiness of Christ, as to its communication, source and attraction. In His company we may know our calling as saints, and be separated from the world by the attractions of His moral beauty. To know the inexorable claim of His death is to find that to live is Christ and to die, gain. Lastly, to fill our hands with service as He shall appoint, doing whatsoever is done in the name of the Lord Jesus, yielding in spirit, soul and body to God, this is the true sanctification of *'mala yad'*. There can be no reserve in this, for it has been well said, "Genuine consecration reaches not only the service of a man's hand and lips, but involves his substance also". It cannot be partial, to be real it must be entire. "I beseech you therefore, brethren, by the compassion of God, to present your bodies a living sacrifice, holy, acceptable to God, which is your intelligent service" (Romans 12:1, J.N.D.).

Figure 17: The covering of badger skins

### THE BADGER SKINS

This was the final exterior covering, all that was beautiful and valuable was beneath. The mere onlooker would see nothing to attract in the outward appearance of the Tabernacle. It was so when the Son of God was amongst men, and those too His own people, in whom some discernment might have been expected. When they saw Him there was no beauty that they should desire Him. In all that He was, He cut clean across the popular ideal, He was a separate Man. He was such because of His consecration to God, for the badger skins resting upon the rams' skins, and like them without dimension, point the lesson that if separation does not flow from consecration, it is not only valueless in God's sight but an offence to Him. Such was and is the separation of the Pharisee. The word 'Pharisee' comes from the Hebrew word '*parash*' meaning 'to separate', and it has been thought that when Paul in Romans 1:1 speaks of himself as 'separated' unto the Gospel of God, he tacitly alluded by way of contrast to that which had formerly been his manner of life, when after the straightest sect of the Jews' religion he lived a Pharisee

{Acts 26:5}. How easily may that which begins in real devotion to God, if not maintained by personal communion, degenerate into the simple designation of a class devoid of living power. It was so with those who bore the name of Pharisee. Their origin was during a state of indifference to the claims of God amongst the returned Jews from the captivity, such as the prophet Malachi describes. They were faithful amidst the faithless, and they received the name of the 'separated' in recognition of the firm stand which they made against the general tendencies of their time. But whatever their first intention may have been, if they began in the spirit it was not long before they sought to be made perfect through the flesh. Their name thus lost its honourable meaning, as frequently, alas! happens with movements which consist only in a protest against prevailing evils. "Thou hast a name that thou livest, and art dead." How different was the path of Him Whom the badger skins typify: unswerving vigilance in the defence and safeguarding of the truth, resisting every approach of evil, repelling and overcoming it, and that in presence of temptation, contradiction, pressure and persecution.

To all this there was no measure, it was absolute. Faith saw beneath this the beauty of His character and the exquisite blending of truth and grace. Those who gave, not a mere passing glance, but contemplated Him, saw His glory as the only begotten of the Father. But if they were thus to behold Him as the chosen of God and precious, it could not be apart from sharing His rejection as disallowed indeed of men.

Regarding what animal is intended by the Hebrew word '*tachash*' (Revised Version 'sealskin') there is some difficulty. The word occurs again in Ezekiel 16:10 where it is evidently a material for ornamental sandals. The

Septuagint and Vulgate regard the word *'tachash'* as the name of common leather dyed some particular colour, Septuagint 'blue skins' (hyacinthine). F. W. Grant renders it 'seals' and this perhaps is the most likely, the Hebrew word bearing a close resemblance to the Arabic *'tuchash'*, a general name for the dolphins, porpoises and seals abounding in the Red Sea. The badger is common in Palestine but it is difficult to see how the skins of so small an animal could have been obtained in sufficient numbers.

The overruling thought in the use of the material was evidently protection, for it was used not only for the Tabernacle exterior, but as a covering for the ark, lampstand, table, incense and brazen altars.

To summarise the curtains and coverings:-

- Badger (seal) skins set forth Christ as a *Separate* Man.
- Rams' skins set forth Christ as a *Devoted* Man.
- Goats' hair sets forth Christ as a *Suffering* Man.
- Linen, colour & cherubim set forth Christ as a *Glorious* Man.

## Chapter 17: The Vail, The Door, and The Gate

Before leaving the fabrics, a few words may be added to that which has already been remarked upon the three entrances, for they represent three distinct experiences in the soul's approach to God: three appropriations of the greatness of Christ.

1. In the gate of the Court, Christ is seen as 'The Way'.
2. In the door of the Tabernacle, Christ is seen as 'The Truth'.
3. In the vail of the Holiest, Christ is seen as 'The Life'.

The Gate proclaims pre-eminent grace.

The Door proclaims the gospel of the glory of Christ.

The Vail proclaims Him Who is the image of God.

The first is the gospel which leads into the court of Levitical service connected with cleansing. In knowing Christ as 'The Way', the only way of salvation for sinners, the soul becomes very anxious to spread the good news of the value of the cleansing blood. This is the fundamental truth found in the epistle to the Romans, and good it is when this foundation is solidly laid in faith, and good is that eager desire for the salvation of the lost by a way so blessed and effectual.

The second entrance leads the soul to know Christ as the summing up of all truth. If the first relates to the babes in the family of God, this would connect itself with the young men who are strong and in whom the word of God abides, and have overcome the wicked one, for they have come into the presence of Him Who is the Light of Life and the Bread of Life. Knowing Him thus, they are already over Jordan as risen with Christ. It is the note struck in the epistle to Colossae.

But how shall we speak of the Vail[31] which Hebrews 10:20 tells us is His flesh through which is an open way into the Holiest of all.

As long as the Lord Jesus was in the flesh, His presence declared the impossibility of anyone approaching God, except Himself.

We can readily understand the court of service where we are to diligently follow every good work and as we have opportunity, make known to sinners the way of salvation and minister to the bodily needs of our brethren and neighbours. We may be numbered amongst the ranks of the valiants for the truth and stand firm against the subtle attacks of the enemy to corrupt or neutralise it by human philosophy, but is not the Holiest of all an untrodden place to the majority of Christian people. In the Gate and the Door the

---

31 The Hebrew word translated 'vail' is derived from an unusual root signifying 'to break', in a secondary sense 'to separate' and only used of the vail, {'*poreketh*'}.

presentation of Christ to men is seen in the needlework upon the one side only, but in the Vail it is what He is also to God, for it is made of cunning work, both sides alike. We may well wonder to find the way open, and liberty given to enter into the innermost recess of God's secret place, there only to adore, and there where Jesus, Jesus only is seen, to lay our tribute of praise and worship at His feet. It is the highest occupation to which the creature can be called. Then also there to hear such communications as the Ephesian epistle affords, such is the holy privilege of those who have known Him that is from the beginning. Through the rent Vail, rent by the one offering of His Son, cleansed by blood and water, Altar and Laver, we may draw near.

God our Saviour, Man from Heaven,
  Lamb Whose precious blood
Tells that we are white and stainless
  In the eyes of God;
We adore Thee, free to enter
  Thy most holy place,
Brought to Love's eternal centre,
  Pure before Thy Face.
There, O God, our hearts adore Thee,
  Where Thou fain wouldst be;
Thou in us, O Love Eternal!
  We in Thee.[32]

32 Frances Bevan, "*The Last Parable of Ezekiel*", Chapter X, *The Secret of His Tabernacle*, London: Chas. J. Thynne, 1900

| | |
|---|---|
| The Court … | If any man serve Me (John 12:26). |
| The Holy … | I will manifest Myself to him (John 14:21). |
| The Holiest … | We will make our abode with him (John 14:23). |

Thus the Vail speaks to us of Christ 'The Life', the life eternal, deathless, unchanging, of joy unutterable, of bliss untold, the Holiest where saints still on earth may enter, the place where those who have departed to be with Christ are. There in that third heaven, the paradise of God, they see His face and hear from His lips things that no human language can convey. Yet even now the Spirit's power gives the foretaste of that offering of priestly service to hearts to whom Christ is all in all, the inexhaustible, unchanging source of all life and joy, with Whom is no variableness nor shadow of turning.

## Chapter 18:
## The Golden Vessels of the Sanctuary

These were four in number, the *Ark* placed in the Holiest, and the *Table, Lampstand* and *Censer* in the Holy.

In three of these, the Ark, Table and Censer, or Incense Altar, the materials of which they were formed were Gold and Acacia wood.

The gold speaks plainly of our Lord in every attribute of Deity, whilst the wood as clearly presents Him as perfectly human in every essential part of humanity, spirit, soul and body. In His person incomprehensible, being both God and man. It must be remembered that we are considering the patterns of things as seen in the heavens, hence we have the opposite of what was evident in the day of the humiliation of our Lord. Then it was the wood that covered the gold, and faith discerned the Divine glory beneath it. Here however we gaze upon Him, the Son of Man glorified, hence the gold is upon the wood. The Lampstand is entirely of gold. Everything speaks of glory revealed in the light of the Holy Spirit, for within the Tabernacle all the illumination came from the seven lamps upon the Lampstand, and the manifestation of the Divine Presence upon the Ark.

### The Table of Shewbread

In Exodus 25:23-30 the description of the Table is given, but for the shewbread we must turn to Leviticus 24:5. The Table is typical wholly of Christ, but the bread, whilst presenting Him as the food of His priests, also shows the place they have as supported by Him in the presence of God.

The dimensions of the Table were 2 cubits in length, 1 cubit in breadth, 1½ cubits in height.[33] No thickness is given, pointing to a mystery beyond the creature's ken, to the name which no man knows but He Himself (Revelation 19:12). In His person He is 'secret' (Judges 13:18). He is 'Wonderful' (Isaiah 9:6). The 2 cubits relate to the witness God has borne to His Son; the 1 cubit to the Divine purpose concerning Him, and the 1½ cubits, as in the case of the boards, reminding us of His rejection and death.

A table is evidently designed to bear something upon it, so that we are led to the thought of Christ supporting and maintaining His Own in the Divine Presence. Around the edge of the table was a crown of gold, a witness to the security of this position, the loaves being

---

33 The *length* was equal to the space between the pillars of the door, 2 cubits, and equal to the height of the incense altar. The *breadth* was equal to that of the incense altar. The *height* was equal to that of the grate of the altar of burnt offering from the ground to the width of the boards, and the height of the Ark, 1½ cubits.
The bread of communion is on the same level as the entrance, propitiation and acceptance we have in Christ (1 John 4:17).
The length and breadth of the Table are less than the Ark, for there is ever more in Christ in His relation Godward than in His relation to His people.

Figure 18: The Table of Shewbread

preserved from disarrangement or falling during the wilderness journey.[34]

Appropriate to this, four golden rings, telling of Divine love, were placed immediately under this crown for places for the staves, typical of strength. Outside the table a border was made, a handbreadth in width and this also had a crown of gold, in this case speaking of separation, for if the nearness of the saints in Christ to God is to be known and enjoyed there must be a corresponding distance from the world. What is to be the measure of our separation? Does it not speak to us of the claim of the pierced Hand that has brought us to the Father, and does it not tell of the Hand of His love that holds all His children. We are clearly assured in

---

34 The word for 'crown' in the text is nowhere used in Scripture to denote the crown of royalty:
{*'zar'*} on the golden vessels only.
{*'nezer'*} the plate on the mitre, a crown of royalty (2 Kings 11:12).
{*'kether'*} a circlet or diadem, see Esther {1:11, 2:17}.

John 10:28-29 of this double security, where our Lord tells us that no one can pluck His sheep out of *His* hand, and further adds, "None can pluck them out of *My Father's* hand".

The word used for the Table is '*shulchan*' which comes from a root meaning 'to stretch out, extend' and from the same root comes the word '*siloam*' — 'sent', as in John 9:7. Into the hand of the Sent One of God the sheep have been committed, and we are well assured that of all that the Father has given Him not one will be lost.

### The loaves

The loaves upon the Table call for very distinct attention. The number 12 naturally takes our thoughts to the tribes of Israel, and rightly so, for to them belong the administration which, in connection with a reigning Christ, shall fill the earth with the knowledge of God, and by whom the fragrance of His name shall be spread abroad (note the incense upon the loaves {Leviticus 24:7}), but this can only be when they as a nation shall accord Him the place which, at His first coming, they refused to Him.

The-word 'shewbread' is taken from the Vulgate and the German of Luther; in Scripture it is known as 'face bread' or 'bread of faces'; it was the bread set in the presence of God (Exodus 25:30, 35:13, 39:36). (The Jews suppose that 'faces' indicates that the loaves were square.)

In Exodus 25:30, 'me' = 'my face' ('*panim l'phanai*'). In Numbers 4:7 it is called 'the continual bread' or 'table of the presence'; in 1 Samuel 21:4, 6, 'the hallowed bread', that is, when removed from the table it was set apart for priestly use. In 1 Chronicles 9:32 it is called in the

### The number 12

- The stones in Jordan.
- The shoulder stones & breastplate.
- Patriarchs & apostles.
- Foundations of the heavenly city.
- Fruit of the tree of Life.
- 120 names in Acts 1 = 12 × 10.
- The courses of the priests and singers — 24 = 12 × 2 (1 Chronicles 24, 25).
- The captains of Israel, each over 24,000 (1 Chronicles 27:1-15).

| | |
|---|---|
| 12 loaves | Leviticus 24:5-6 |
| 2 loaves | Leviticus 23:17 |
| 1 loaf | 1 Corinthians 10:16-17<br>That which represents Christ sets forth also His people. |

{Authorized Version} margin 'bread of ordering', also in 2 Chronicles 13:11. In Nehemiah 10:33 'the sets of bread' are spoken of, whilst in Hebrews 9:2 it is referred to as 'Bread of setting forth, or presentation'.

It is in Leviticus 24:5-9 that the detail of the loaves is given, and in verse 7 it is known as 'Bread of remembrance' or 'Bread for a memorial'. It is Christ that is pre-eminently all this, the One upon whom the eye of God rests with infinite delight and Whose incense is ever a savour of peace, and a witness of the coming glory of His coming as Prince of Peace. Such was the import of the frankincense which was put upon the loaves and which was burnt wholly for God when the loaves were changed every Sabbath.

'Bread of faces' gives the idea of that close personal intimacy which lies in the term 'face to face'. The face of God shone on the face of the loaves, whilst the face of the bread looked up into the face of God. Such was Christ's joy, and such may be ours. It is significant that in Exodus 25 nothing is said of the number of the loaves, the bread is viewed as a whole, presenting what Christ is to God.

In Leviticus 24:5 the material and weight of the loaves is given. They were to be of fine flour, baked, similar to the meal offering of Leviticus 2. No mention is made of leaven as in the case of the two wave loaves of Pentecost (Leviticus 23:17), representative of Jew and Gentile. The fine flour represents the perfect humanity of our Lord Jesus Christ. In Him there was no unevenness, no predominant quality to produce the effect of a distinctive character such as was exhibited in the energy and zeal of Paul, the ardent affection of Peter, or the abstraction of thought and tender sensibilities of John. In the Lord Jesus all these blended in perfect harmony. There was nothing salient because all was in perfect subjection to God. Each character in Him exactly did its service and then disappeared. When meekness became Him, He was meek; when indignation, who could stand before His rebuke?

The loaves were baked, subjected to the action of fire. The Hebrew word for cakes is '*challoth*' from '*chalal*', to pierce, to wound to death. ('*challoth*' is translated 'slain' in Genesis 34:27 and in Numbers 19:16, 18.) The natural effect of this piercing would be that the fire could penetrate every part. As these cakes speak of Christ, the piercing points not primarily to His death, but to the constant subjection of His whole being to the heated fire of trial, and the searching of God's holy Word.

Two tenth *deals* {or *ephah*} of fine flour went to each loaf. One tenth deal equals one *omer* = 5 pounds, so that each loaf or cake weighed ten pounds. This was twice the daily supply of manna for each person. There is much more in Christ than that which suffices for our need.

The loaves were placed in two rows, six in a row. It has been thought that this implied two piles of six each, but this could scarcely be, as such an arrangement could hardly be described as a row, and the frankincense would not have been on each loaf. The table is spoken of as pure, the frankincense also, so carefully does God guard the holy person of His Son, in types that speak of His humanity. The bread was placed hot upon the table every Sabbath (Leviticus 24:8, 1 Samuel 21:6, 1 Chronicles 9:32). The frankincense was removed and burnt to God as an offering made by fire, and in the fragrance of this the children of Israel are seen in connection with the purpose of God relating to the everlasting covenant. The Sabbath day prefigures the rest of God when it shall be revealed that God has formed the people for Himself and they shall show forth His praise.

Only two priestly activities are enjoined for the Sabbath:–

1. The burnt offering with its meat and drink offering, (Numbers 28:9-10), figurative of the ground on which the rest of God will be brought in.

2. The arranging of the shewbread, showing the Divine order in which Israel will appear in that day.

Note the seal of this in the fourfold repetition of 'Jehovah' (Leviticus 24:6-9).

The border of an handbreadth round the table calls for one or two further remarks. The word {'*misgereth*'} primarily means 'an enclosure' so 'a fortress' or close place (Psalm 18:45). As a type of Christ, the bread is fenced off from all other, and this is important because the holy humanity of Christ was after an heavenly order, and it was not derived from the first man who was of the earth, earthy. The border excluded all thought of this, excluding all that was not consistent with the glory of Christ. His people bear the same heavenly character and we may read John 17 in the light of the two crowns of the table, the crown of Sonship and the crown of Separation, and note the recurrence of 'glory', 'glorify', 'kept' and 'keep'.

Removed from the table, the bread became the food of the priests, and this opens up a subject of exceeding interest and importance. The Divine life imparted to us is dependent upon support. True, that sustainment never fails on the side of Christ, but on the side of present communion, joy, and strength, there is the need of continual appropriation and feeding upon Him, and His own hand has spread a table for us in the wilderness, indeed in the presence of all that is enmity to us (Psalm 23:5).

Three figures are afforded in Scripture in relation to eating of the Divine provision: the Manna, the Old Corn of the Land, and the Shewbread, each of these being characteristic of how Christ becomes our food.

The *Manna* was provision for the wilderness, a daily necessity for the circumstances of the way. It was typical of the true bread from heaven, that is Christ once humbled here. It was small, round, white, in taste like honey, a lovely simile of the grace that we assimilate as we daily sit at His feet. In His presence we are rested and calmed; instead of the corners that irritate, we discover the roundness that does not chafe and fret. Then as we listen to the words none other could utter, how sweet are they to our taste, yea sweeter than honey and the honeycomb, the fresh oil of His Spirit blending all circumstances into the consciousness of one great good. The food we partake of becomes by assimilation part of our very selves, and we take character from that upon which we feed. So it is with him in whom Christ, received by personal faith, abides. He lives by reason of Christ, Christ lives in him, Christ it is Who is the explanation of his life, its thoughts and purpose. Thus it is to possess, to enjoy, to live that which is truly life, a life which abides for ever and over which hangs no shadow of death.

When Israel arrived in the land of promise a new form of sustenance awaited them, the *Old Corn of the Land*. This speaks of a heavenly Christ Who has passed by the way of the cross, out of wilderness circumstances, and stands victorious over the power of death and the grave. To appropriate Him thus is to share the power of His resurrection and triumph and to enter the joy of a justified, victorious life, in identification with Christ to which neither sin nor death can have ought {anything} to say. It is a Christ seated above, Who came from above, Who died and is risen again, and ascended up where He was before, Whom I now know. Risen with Christ, we feed on the old corn of the land, on heavenly things, as our present portion. Such sustainment strengthens us to overcome the world, and transfers our minds to the things above, until Christ Who is our life shall appear, and our identification with Him be manifest to all.

Lastly, the *Shewbread* was the food of the priests. It is Christ as He ever will be, centre of the Father's love and counsel; Head of His body the Church, the continual fulness of Him that filleth all in all; and Leader of the adoring worship with which the joy of God shall fill the eternal ages. The shewbread belonged to the Holy of the presence, upon it the face of God shone, and we on our part may well marvel at the grace which permits us to feed upon the bread of God, the living bread which came down from heaven, that a man may eat thereof and not die.

### Asociated vessels

There were certain vessels upon the Table which appear to connect the loaves upon the Table with the pouring out unto death which was necessary if the bread of life was to become available to us: "Except ye eat the flesh of the Son of Man and drink His blood ye have no life in you" {John 6:53}.

There were dishes (*kearothaiv*) to carry the loaves to and from the table; they are suggestive of the offering of the body of Jesus Christ. There were spoons (*cappothaiv*) for the placing of the frankincense, telling of the fragrance that ascended to God from the offering. There were bowls or cups (*menakkiyothaiv*) reminding us of the cup of sorrow which our Lord took from the Father's hand, which has become to us the cup of blessing. Lastly there were covers, or rather, flagons to pour out withal (Exodus 25:29 {Authorized Version} margin) (*kesothaiv*), expressive of the outpouring before God of joy and praise, the drink offering which it is the privilege of God's priesthood to bring to Him.

On the march the Table and its furniture were covered, and it then became typical of the communion of saints concerning the perfections of Christ. The loaves were removed and upon the Table was spread a cloth of blue. It is the Sent One from heaven Who is the basis of communion. Upon this the spoons, dishes, cups and flagons with the continual bread were placed, signifying the witness of the saints to the life and death of Him Who came from heaven. Over these was put a cloth of scarlet in anticipation of His coming glory; and finally the whole was covered with a covering of badger skins, for protection and preservation from all common or defiling influences {Numbers 4:7-8}.

## The Golden Lampstand

{Described in Exodus 25:31-40,} this stood on the south or left-hand side when entering the Holy of the Tabernacle, whilst opposite to it was the table which we have just been considering.

As in the Table the basic idea was food, so in the Lampstand it is light. The thought of light is connected both with Christ and with the Holy Spirit, the peculiar character of Whose ministry it is to take of the things of Christ and to show them to us, until our hearts, so easily attracted by other things, long to behold the beauty of the Lord. It is of this loveliness that the Lampstand speaks.

The weight of metal employed in its construction is specified, but no measure is spoken of, for what measurement can there be of the Infinite. The material was pure gold, the symbol of the radiant perfection of Him Who is the brightness of the Divine Glory. The weight was one talent (*kikkar*), the meaning of the Hebrew word being 'a circuit', again expressing the thought of that which is eternal, while it was the most costly of all the Tabernacle vessels, being estimated to be worth £6,000 {1934; perhaps £2,500,000 in 2019}. Authorities differ as to the exact equivalent of the Hebrew weights, a talent of gold being heavier than a

Figure 19: The Golden Lampstand

talent of silver, {ranging from 75 pounds to} about 131 pounds.

Its construction was one beaten work, that is the different parts were not made separately and then put together, but the whole was beaten out of one piece of pure gold. Surely we may see the beauty of the Lord in this, for all that He said and did was of one piece with His Deity. Nothing ever contradicted this, never did He commit the slightest error or show ignorance. All was pure gold without alloy, without joining or seam. He was God manifest in flesh, and as we may marvel at the skill needed for such goldsmith's work seen in the Lampstand, we may still more wonder as we contemplate Deity of one piece with the perfection of manhood in our Lord Jesus Christ. Truly no one knows the Son but the Father. The explanation of the mystery of His person must ever remain unsolvable to the creature on earth or in heaven.

"There only to adore, my soul its strength shall find."

Thus the gold, the talent, the one piece tell us, as another has said, "of Him Who is in nature Divine, God over all; in existence eternal, in the beginning He was; in person distinct, yet the same, the *'atta hu'* (Psalm 102:27, Hebrews 1:12), Who changes not."

The design of the Lampstand was one centre column called the shaft, having four sets of triple ornamentation consisting of bowls, knops and flowers. Proceeding out of the shaft were six branches, three on each side, each having three sets of the same triple ornamentation. Three additional knops were placed under the springing of each three pairs of branches. There is no description of any base or stand, again conveying the thought of the indescribable eternal glory from which the Son of God came forth: 'The glory that was His before the world was.'

The predominant number in the Lampstand is 7 — Divine perfection, as also in the sets of ornaments in shafts and branches, 4 and 3. Such is Immanuel, God (3) with us (4). The repetition of the ornamentation, 22 times, adds the thought of recurrence, for in all the ways of God, every end is only a new beginning, each evening ends with a morning, and the end and passing away of the old creation is the introduction of new heavens and a new earth; every evening is the promise of a morning.

The seven lamps placed upon the stand shed their light throughout the Holy, shining upon the table and incense altar, revealing the golden boards, the overhead curtains, and the vail, all speaking of the mediatorial glories of Christ. The immediate object of the lamps however was to illuminate the lampstand, to give light over against the face of it (Exodus 25:37, {Authorized Version} margin) or literally 'upon the sides of its faces'. The lamps and the pure olive oil with which they were fed speak of the Holy Spirit Whose office it is to take of the things of Christ and reveal them to us; and well it is to remind ourselves that these things are not seen by natural light, still less by that light which human intelligence and reason can afford, but God hath revealed them to us by His Spirit.

The significance then of the Lampstand is this:–

> Divine light showing the excellent beauty of Christ in the power of the Spirit.

In shape the Lampstand was a conventional representation of an almond tree. It could scarcely have had the form which the architect of the Arch of Titus gave it, with the seven lamps on one level, for evidently the centre shaft was higher than the branches, and these though equal to each in length commenced one below the other. But why an almond tree? To begin with the almond is prominent on shaft and branches, and the meaning of the Hebrew word for almond '*shaqued*' will lead us to the answer. The word means 'to be wakeful', 'to hasten', from a root 'to be sleepless'. Therefore the Hebrews called the almond the wakener tree, since it is the first to blossom after the sleep of winter.

In Jeremiah 1:11-12 we may see how the word is used both as a verb and a substantive. In reply to Jehovah's question, "What seest thou?" the prophet replies, "I see a rod of an *almond* tree." The Lord answers, "I will *hasten* my word to perform it." Literally it is "I see the rod of a *shaqued* tree," and the reply is "I will *shaqued* my word to perform it." In Psalm 127:1 the word is translated 'waketh', but the incident that conveys the significance of the almond most clearly is in Numbers 17. It was after the rebellion of Korah, Dathan and Abiram that, in order to quite take away occasion of murmuring amongst the children of Israel, and to definitely mark the priesthood by the symbol of resurrection, God commanded the heads of the tribes to bring each man a rod according to the house of their fathers, and to write his name upon the rod of his tribe, and to put upon the rod of the tribe of Levi the name of Aaron. They did so and laid them up over night in the Tabernacle of the Congregation, 12 sticks, hard, dry and dead. In the morning 11 of the rods were found as they had been put, no change had taken place. In the case however of Aaron's rod, life had come from the dead wood. It had budded, and brought forth buds and bloomed blossoms and yielded almonds, providing a beautiful figure of resurrection, and pointing forwards to the priesthood of our Lord.

The figure of the almond tree opens to our vision a risen Christ Who has gone in to God as our great High Priest.

Knops (*kaphtohr*) or *buds*, flowers or *blossoms* (*perach*), almonds or *fruit* (*shakad*) such was the ornamentation repeated 22 times, twice the number marking the sin offering. In these three symbols we may discern the past, present and future in relation to our Lord and the Spirit's witness thereto.

The Lord's life on earth may be likened to the bud which contains within itself the coming flower and subsequent fruit, all there but as yet undeveloped. "I have {yet} many things to say unto you, but ye cannot bear them now" {John 16:12}, and again, "These things understood not His disciples at the first" {John 12:16}, and again, "All things which Jesus *began* both to do and to teach" {Acts 1:1, J.N.D.}. The opening of the understanding to the import of that which they had heard, was the first action of the Comforter, the Holy Spirit from the Father. "He shall teach you all things and bring all things to your remembrance, whatsoever I have said unto you" (John 14:26). Precious indeed beyond words was all that He said and did when here, and it is not surprising that the witness of God to this is seen in the three added knops under the three pairs of branches. In the four Gospels is recorded all that was brought to the remembrance of the apostles of that path of shining light that, uncheered by earthly smiles, led only to the cross, but in which there lay a revelation beyond words, the revelation of the Father, the Word of Life: heard, seen, contemplated and handled by the men who conveyed it to us in Spirit-taught words, that our joy might be full.

But how fragrant the flower! In John 15:26 our Lord told His disciples that when the Comforter came, He would have even more to communicate: "He shall testify of Me". The witness of the Spirit concerns the present glory of our Lord, as risen and ascended, and all the present truth connected with Him seated above. It was all this that Paul desired so earnestly to lead the believers into in his letter to the Hebrews. He wished them to reach out to perfection, to have their hearts attracted to Christ, a Man in the glory of God, seeing Him by faith in the place of God's purpose for man, that they might learn that by the same Spirit they were united to Him and would be morally conformed to Him when He comes forth. The bride in Song of Solomon 1:14 could say, "My beloved is unto me as a cluster of camphire (henna flowers)". It is the sight of a glorified Christ that dims this world's fading glory, and it is this that the Holy Spirit reveals to us in the Epistles. It is an added fragrance to His path of sorrow, the remembrance of which we can never forget, even as again in Song of Solomon 1:13, "A bundle of myrrh is my well-beloved unto me; he shall lie all night betwixt my breasts". So may Christ, both suffering and glorified, abide in the affections of His saints, during the night of His absence.

But what of the fruit? Bowls (cups, R.V.), made like unto almonds; the word *'gahbia'* = a bowl, also a calyx, the evidence as it surrounds the base of the fruit, of the previous blossom. So in the coming day of Christ's glory when He shall see the fruit of the travail of His soul, He will always be the Heavenly One to His Church and she ever to Him as a bride adorned for her husband.

In John 16:13, the Spirit's work is to reveal things to come, to give a vision of the things hoped for, the coming glory that shall fill the heavens and the earth; the great Hallelujah, that as the voice of a great multitude, and as the voice of many waters, and as the voice of mighty thunderings, shall proclaim the Lord God omnipotent reigneth. All things shall be headed up in the Man Who endured the cross, the fruit of which shall be the presentation to the Father of a sinless universe, in which 'God shall be all in all'.

The branches of the Lampstand have yet more to show us as the Spirit shall enlighten us of the glory of Christ. It would appear that the seven branches of the Lampstand were in the mind of the prophet Isaiah when he wrote Isaiah 11:2. The centre shaft will correspond with the first sentence, 'The Spirit of the Lord shall rest upon Him'. The first pair of branches corresponds to 'The Spirit of wisdom and understanding'; the centre pair to 'The Spirit of counsel and might'; the lower pair to 'The Spirit of knowledge and of the fear of the Lord'.

In the centre shaft Christ is revealed as the Anointed of the Lord. Marked out as Messiah, saluted as the beloved Son at His baptism, the Spirit of the Lord bore witness to all He said and did, so that to speak injuriously of Him was to blaspheme against the Holy Spirit.

The spirit of wisdom and understanding or discernment characterised Him in all things. His enemies could not resist it, nor stand before His searching gaze. He ever saw below the surface, and was equal to every emergency. Truly His words were as deep waters and the well spring of His wisdom as a flowing brook. Hypocrisy shunned His presence or was scathingly exposed, whilst wisdom's children sat at His feet and heard His word.

Then His counsel was not like that of men, who are unable to carry out that which they propose. His word was with power and might; and ever in exercise towards the poor and needy, each act adding lustre to His name of "Counsellor, The Mighty God" (Isaiah 9:6), and displaying Him "Wonderful in counsel" and "Excellent in working" (Isaiah 28:29).

In the lower pair of branches connected with the spirit of knowledge and the fear of the Lord, the underlying principles of the path of our Lord are revealed. He lived in the absolute good of the knowledge of God and the discernment of His perfect will. There are many words for 'knowledge' in Hebrew. The word used here, '*dah-ath*', tells of that capacity for discerning God, which results in the governing of all conduct by His will. This is the true 'Fear of the Lord'. Psalm 119 is a beautiful expression of the fear of the Lord which is the true wisdom, and the knowledge of the holy which is understanding.

Seven lamps stood upon the Lampstand, fed with pure olive oil every evening by the High Priest (Exodus 30:8, Leviticus 24:1-4). Oil is a type of the Holy Spirit; in the Divine System the Holy Spirit is the only source of light. The seven lamps were the perfection of testimony to Christ risen, with which we may compare the seven witnesses of the resurrection in 1 Corinthians 15:4-8. The same perfection of the Spirit will be seen in heaven (Revelation 4:5).

At the first, the care and service of the maintenance of the light was entrusted to Aaron and his sons (Exodus 27:20-21), but after the failure and sin of Aaron's sons, it pertained to Aaron alone to light the lamps. However the saints, the priestly family, may fail and prove themselves unworthy of their office, the light shines forth for the eye of God, maintained unfailingly by the hand of a greater priest than Aaron, by Him Who abides a Priest for ever after the order of Melchisedek. It is during the night of Christ's rejection that the lampstand fulfils its purpose, therefore in the millennial temple that Ezekiel describes, there is no such vessel; no ark, for Christ will be present; no table of shewbread seen in the light of the lamps, for all Israel will be saved; no laver, for no more will hands and feet be soiled; only the two altars are there, for the sacrifice shall never be forgotten, and worship shall be a constant employ.

There were certain instruments connected with the Lampstand: *snuffers* {*melqach*}, same word translated 'tongs' in {Authorized Version} Exodus 25:38; and *snuffdishes* {*machtah*}. Each day revealed the freshness of the light which shone forth from our Lord and each day we may experience the renewing of the Holy Spirit by Whom alone there can be the outshining of the knowledge of God in the face of Jesus Christ.

There were therefore provided Golden Snuffers to remove that which had yielded the service of the light. Consumed in holy zeal for God, the prophet records of Him, "He wakeneth morning by morning, he wakeneth mine ear to hear as the learner" {Isaiah 50:4}.

But nothing was lost and there were Golden Snuff Dishes. Nothing was forgotten and the past service was carefully preserved by Divine care. The Holy Spirit has gathered the details of the shining forth of God in Christ, for ever to abide to His glory.

Finally, *coverings* were provided {Numbers 4:9-10}. The Lampstand and its instruments, with the oil vessels, were put in a cloth of blue, a witness that Christ has passed into the heavens and that all connected with Him are heavenly. Then came the protective, separating cover of badger skins, for the world has nothing to say to this, and the presence of the Spirit but convicts the world of sin, righteousness and judgment to come. The Light of the world has left it, and the world walks in darkness and knows not whither it goeth.

No staves, but a *bar or bearing frame* was specified {Numbers 4:10}, which appears to emphasize the special character of the Lampstand as belonging only to God, and His witness by and in the Spirit.

In Solomon's temple there were ten lampstands, significant, no doubt, of the Spirit's witness in the Millennium to the glory of Christ and the outpouring of the Spirit upon all flesh (Joel 2:28-29). In that temple all the holy vessels of the Tabernacle were deposited (1 Kings 8:4), remaining there until they were carried to Babylon by Nebuchadnezzar (Jeremiah 52:18-19). There, in the midst of the orgies of a feast with which Belshazzar had associated the golden vessels of the sanctuary, the fingers of a man's hand wrote upon the wall, over against the lampstand, the Divine sentence against the impious king who had insulted Him.

Before leaving the subject of the Lampstand, allusion may be made to three occasions in which the figure is carried on. In Zechariah 4:1-10, the prophet beholds a lampstand like the one in the Tabernacle, but with certain additional features. A golden bowl is seen at the top from which the oil flows to the seven lamps through seven golden pipes. This bowl is kept supplied with oil by two olive trees on either side which pour oil into it through two golden pipes. The construction was Divine for no other material than gold is mentioned. The vision represents the living supply of the Spirit in perpetual maintenance of the Royalty and Priesthood of Christ. The golden bowl is significant of Christ risen, from Whom all authority and worship is sustained. It is the perfect order that God is going to establish in the earth when Christ sits as Priest upon His throne.

In Revelation 11:3-4, the two witnesses are seen connected with the two olive trees, maintaining the testimony in days of apostacy to the coming King and Priest, a sufficient witness to His advent.

In Revelation 1:12, seven lampstands are seen, representing the assemblies during Christ's absence as distinct light-bearers in their place of service and position of witnesses for Him in the world. They are viewed in their proper character as of God, all of gold. For however they may fail to carry out that for which they have been formed and placed, and are consequently judged, they were founded originally by the Divine Hand.

The oil used in the service of the Tabernacle, whether for light or anointing, was of vegetable origin, 'pure olive oil'. None derived from animal or mineral sources was admissible. The latter was never used, the former, the fat, was wholly burnt upon the altar. It was obtained by the death of the animal and was typical of the intrinsic excellence and richness of the offering of Christ to God. Both fat and blood were expressly forbidden as articles of food.

Olive oil was used for the purpose of anointing, for light, and for the preparation of that which was to be eaten. In these three ways it was typical of the Holy Spirit by Whom kings and priests were consecrated, from Whom all light comes, and without Whom there can be no assimilation of food which God provides.

The first mentions of oil are in connection with anointing (Genesis 28:18 and 35:14). The next are in connection with light (Exodus 25:6 and 27:20), and the following (Exodus 29:2) in the preparation of the unleavened cakes.

That the lamps were to burn 'always' means that they were to burn with regularity. The lamps were to be ordered from 'evening to morning', there is no thought of their being alight in the day-time.

Before proceeding to the consideration of the golden altar, it will be appropriate to dwell upon the composition of the oil of holy ointment which was to be compounded after the art of the apothecary.

### The Holy Anointing Oil

The prescription for this is in Exodus 30:22-33 with directions for its use. It was compounded of principal or chief spices. No ordinary ingredient could form part of that which was to typify the moral fragrance of God's beloved Son. The proportions were to be weighed after the shekel of the sanctuary, suited to the estimation of God: Myrrh 500, Cinnamon 250, Calamus 250, Cassia 500, Olive Oil 1 hin.

It will be noticed that the weight of the spices have the factors 5 and 2: $5\times5\times5\times2\times2 = 500$; $5\times5\times5\times2 = 250$. The three 5s show the relation to Christ in man's condition under the eye of God and 2 shows the witness of His approval.

*Myrrh* (*mowr*) is a gum from a dwarf tree of the terebinth family growing in Arabia. Its fragrance[35] is referred to in Song of Solomon 1:13, Psalm 45:8, and Song of Solomon 3:6. The word {translated} 'pure' {*derowr*} is literally 'free' or possibly 'liquid'. It is frequently translated 'liberty' in Scripture[36], this being characteristic of its free flowing from incisions made in the tree. *Mowr* (myrrh) comes from the root word '*marah*' which has the double meaning of 'to trickle in drops' and 'to be bitter', figuratively used in the sense of suffering; compare Ruth 1:20 and 'Smyrna' (Revelation 2:8-11). In type this ingredient of the ointment speaks of the fragrance of our Lord's devotion to the will of God, even to the suffering of death. It was fully exhibited in Gethsemane, 'His sweat was as it were great drops of blood falling down to the ground'; 'Nevertheless, Father, – Not My will but Thine be done' {Luke 22:44, 42}.

The fourth ingredient, *cassia*, (*kiddah*), the mention of which occurs only once more in Scripture (Ezekiel 27:19) is the inner bark of the tree which yields it, stripped off and dried. (Cassia in Psalm 45:8 is another word, '*kaw-tsah*', which means that which is peeled or scraped off, and may refer to the same drug.) It is allied both to cinnamon and senna. The word '*kiddah*' is from a root word meaning 'to cleave', 'to stoop', 'to bow down'. The Septuagint translates it as 'iris' or 'orris root'. It was used in the same proportion as the myrrh, 500 shekels, and, bearing the above in mind, would appear to indicate the pungent, heart-searching detection and refusal of evil, which involved the suffering (myrrh)

35 {*mowr*} 'fragrance': Song of Solomon 4:14, 3:6, 5:5 {and} 13; Proverbs 7:17; Esther 2:12; compare also Matthew 2:11; John 19:39.

36 {*derowr*} translated 'liberty': Leviticus 25:10; Isaiah 61:1; Jeremiah 34:8, 15, 17; Ezekiel 46:17.

necessary to remove it according to the holiness of God. Then the thought of the subsequent bowing down in worship is spiritually appropriate, for the priesthood of our Lord is based upon the sufferings He endured; so that the equal weight of myrrh and cassia would indicate the answer which glory has provided to the suffering of the Cross. "Who for the joy that was set before Him endured the cross" (Hebrews 12{:2}). Or again, as the New Translation reads Psalm 45:8, "Myrrh and aloes, cassia, are all thy garments; out of ivory palaces stringed instruments have made thee glad" {J.N.D.}. Into the joy of heaven Christ has carried the fragrance of His anointing. See also {Psalm 45} verse 7.

The second and third ingredients appear to be included in the designation 'aloes' in Psalm 45 and both are marked out as being 'sweet', and each of the same weight, 250 shekels. Aloes was the inner wood or heart of the tree that grew in India, exceedingly fragrant, worth more than its weight in gold and said to be a sovereign cordial for all fainting fits and nervous disorders. There certainly could not be a better description of the love of Christ, in which are combined the virtues of both cinnamon and calamus, each of which bears the designation, sweet.

Sweet *cinnamon* (*kinnemon besem*) is properly cinnamon of spice, or aromatic cinnamon. The derivation of the word is probably from '*kinna*' = 'jealousy', which comes from a root meaning 'to glow, or burn, or be zealous', added to which is the affix '*min*' = 'form or appearance'. Such was this grace in our Lord, His disciples saw its appearance in Him and remembered that it was written, "The zeal of Thine house hath eaten me up" {John 2:17}. There was exhibited in Christ that ardent zeal for the honour of

God, which however never carried Him out of the current of God's will and ways. What sweet fragrance must such a characteristic have afforded.

Sweet *calamus*, or cane of spice (*keneh besem*).The English word 'cane' is almost identical with the Hebrew '*keneh*'[37] and its Greek and Latin equivalents '*canna*'. The root word means 'to stand upright', hence a cane or reed. Its sweetness as in the case of cinnamon denotes fragrance. It usually grows in miry soil, hence we may read in this ingredient the personal upright righteousness of our Lord, growing out of the miry surroundings of earth.

Lastly the *oil* speaks of the wonderful blending and exhibition of the graces of Christ in the Holy Spirit. He was God's anointed Man, Messiah and Christ, emitting the fragrance of moral perfection both towards God and man, ever delightful to the former and rejected by the latter. The graces of the Spirit in Isaiah 11:2 bear an analogy to the proportions of the spices and oil.

| | | |
|---|---|---|
| 1 hin | of oil olive | – The Spirit of the Lord |
| 500 | of myrrh | – wisdom and understanding |
| 250 | of cinnamon | – counsel |
| 250 | of calamus | – might |
| 500 | of cassia | – knowledge and the fear of the Lord. |

There is the possibility that the *spikenard* of Scripture corresponds to the sweet calamus. A grass or cane grows in India from which is distilled an essential oil, fragrant and prized for its value as a medicine: this is the Indian *nard*. Modern spikenard which is also valuable as a medicine is not a grass but a valerian, the odour of which can hardly be called fragrant.

37 '*keneh*' translated stalk, branch, reed, sweet cane, balance, measuring reed or rod.

The preparation of the ointment pertained to the sons of the priests (1 Chronicles 9:30).

The equivalent weight of spices, 1500 shekels, namely ½ a talent estimated at 65½ pounds, a hin of oil being equal to 1 gallon.

## The Golden Altar

Before the Vail stood the altar to burn incense upon {Exodus 30:1-10}. It was constructed of acacia wood covered with gold, in this resembling the table of shewbread with the same significance of the Deity and humanity of our Lord Jesus Christ. It is called in Ezekiel 41:22, "The table that is before the Lord". Its dimensions, two cubits in height and one cubit in length and breadth, express adequate witness to the Divine purpose fulfilled in Christ. It was foursquare both in relation to its form and also to its position in the second square of 'The Holy', corresponding in this to the brazen altar in the court. Indeed it was only the fire from that altar that might be used to kindle the incense offered on this. All other fire was considered as strange, because not connected with sacrifice. There were four horns indicative of energy and power, and a crown of gold which the Septuagint gives as 'a wreathen border', and the Revised Version (margin) as 'a rim or moulding'. The word used is the same as the crowns upon the table and ark, the thought of separation from all else being prominent; whilst upon the mitre of the high priest, the word used for crown, '*nazar*', is emblematic of royalty and consecration.

There were only two rings to this altar placed at the ribs or meeting of the sides, immediately under the crown. The angles of the altar with the horns would thus point north, south, east and west, a symbol of the world wide worship of the millennial day (Isaiah 66:23, Psalm 65:2).

Figure 20: The Golden Altar

The two rings bear witness to love, without which there can be no real worship acceptable to God. The whole is representative of our Lord as the true worshipper, its connection with the Altar in the court and the Table in the Holy, showing how He associates His Redeemed with Himself in this worship. "In the midst of the assembly I will sing praise unto Thee" (Psalm 22:22, Hebrews 2:12). Upon this altar Aaron was to burn sweet incense every morning when he dressed the lamps, and do the same in the evening when he lit the lamps, or 'caused them to ascend' and this perpetually (Exodus 30:7-8). The connection of the various vessels, including the Laver, the constant use of which was incumbent on the priests in approaching the other vessels, presents us with a five-fold view of the greatness of Christ:

| | | |
|---|---|---|
| 1. | The Brazen Altar | Christ our *Redeemer* |
| 2. | The Laver | Christ our *Sanctification* |
| 3. | The Table of Shewbread | Christ our *Food* |
| 4. | The Lampstand | Christ our *Light* |
| 5. | The Golden Altar | Christ our *Acceptance* |

It is necessary to bear in mind that the Altar of Incense stood in a much closer relation to the Holiest than either the Lampstand or the Table. Its connection with the inner sanctuary is described in language altogether peculiar to itself. It was to be put "Before the vail that is by the ark of the testimony, before the mercy seat that is over the testimony" (Exodus 30:6, compare 40:5, 26; Leviticus 4:7, 18). In 1 Kings 6:22, the altar of incense raised by Solomon is spoken of as "the altar that was by the oracle", while in the vision of John, the place assigned to it in heaven is "before the throne" and "before God" (Revelation 8:3, 9:13). Therefore, although the Altar of Incense stood outside the second vail, it is, in thought at least, fully as much within it as without it. Remembering this may throw light upon the passage in Hebrews 9:4 where, in the enumeration of the vessels, the writer obviously speaks of the altar or golden censer as belonging to the Holiest. Probably this is on account of the rending of the vail, which would bring the altar into the presence of the mercy seat upon the ark in the Holiest. This is truly descriptive of Christian worship, blood having been shed which had rent the vail which no blood of bulls and goats could ever do under the law. It is the privilege of the Christian to have liberty to enter the Holiest by the blood of Jesus, and in spirit now to pass within the vail to offer up spiritual sacrifices of praise and thanksgiving. Although no animal sacrifice was permitted to be laid upon this altar, the incense is distinctly spoken of as 'an offering' (Exodus 30:9).

Yet another important point showing the intimate connection between the golden altar and the Holy of Holies is that in Exodus 30:10 it is called by the same name (*kodesh hakodeshim*) showing that while under the old covenant it was placed outside for use, it really belonged within the vail.

As difficulties have arisen as to what vessel is intended in Hebrews 9:4, it may be said that when the material of which censers were made is referred to in the Old Testament it is always copper. In Revelation 8:3 {and} 5, a golden censer is spoken of, but it is there seen in heaven. The Greek word used for this is '*libanoton*', whereas in Hebrews 9:4 it is the word '*thumiaterion*', which the Septuagint uses for the altar of incense. Strong defines '*thumiaterion*' as a place of fumigation, namely, the altar of incense; with this Delitzch agrees, but Saphir prefers to read 'censer'. The blood of the sin offering was put upon the horns, in acknowledgment that the blood of sacrifice was the only ground of approach to God, this corresponding to the blood sprinkled before and upon the ark in the Holiest. The true vitality of worship and its fragrance to God, must be derived from believing contact with the atoning sacrifice by which the claims of His holiness have been met.

The offering of incense is specifically connected with prayer. The incense which was to be replenished perpetually, symbolized the efficacy and fragrance of Christ, which must ever be recognised as associated with prayer and praise (Psalm 141:2, Hebrews 13:15, compare Revelation 5:8, 8:3-4). In Luke 1 this is distinctly seen. The people are praying without, while Zacharias the priest is offering incense on the golden altar within the Temple. It was on this occasion that the angel appeared to him standing on the right or south side (compare Ezekiel 47:1) between the altar and the lampstand.

The crown upon the altar of incense is the crown of Sonship, the relationship in which the highest character of worship is expressed.

### The Incense

'Take unto thee sweet spices' = fragrant drugs (Exodus 30:34). In the case of ointment it was 'best spices'. The principal thought in the incense is fragrance, note the repetition of 'sweet' or 'fragrant' in verse 34. There were four ingredients blended or salted together in equal proportions. Also notice the multiplication of words in verse 35: a perfume, a confection or seasoning, after the art of the apothecary, tempered or salted, pure, holy — all suggesting a fulness which is found in Christ, blended together by the Spirit of God Who is the true apothecary, producing that concerning which there must be no attempt at imitation.

The Incense is expressive of the fragrance of Christ to God which was for His delight. What outbreakings of desire in Him answering to God's thoughts and purposes of love! His seasons of prayer had a true sanctuary character. Like the altar itself it was *'kodesh hakodeshim'*, and some of it beaten very small was to be put before the Testimony. Thus it was on the Day of Atonement (Leviticus 16) when Aaron entered into the Holy of Holies, he was to do so with his hands full of sweet incense beaten small. This is indicative of the true character of worship, a presentation to God of the excellencies of the grace and character of Christ. It is helpful in this connection to consider the fragrant drugs of which the incense was composed.

*'Stacte'* is the word used by the Septuagint for the Hebrew *'nataph'* = to drop, distil. Frequently it is rendered 'drop' and in the sense of speech 'prophecy' (Ezekiel 20:46, Micah 2:6). It is so called from the drops of gum which exude from the tree which produces it when pierced. It will suggest to us the fragrant outflow of speech, act and life from Christ to God, a fragrance which was accentuated by the enduring of suffering even unto death (compare Luke 4:22, 22:44).

*Onycha* (*shecheleth*), Septuagint *'onux'* = a nail, finger-nail; it is a shell fish found in the Red Sea which yielded a perfume on being crushed. It was also used as a medicine. It recalls the sufferings of Christ, His crushing even unto death, which yielded the fragrance of complete devotedness to God.

> 'Love that on death's dark vale
> Its sweetest odours spread.'

*Galbanum* ({*helbenah*}) is a resinous gum obtained from the East coast of Africa and Arabia. It has a bitter acrid taste and a musty and disagreeable odour, which, however, adds strength and persistence to other ingredients. The word is the same in Hebrew and Greek, and the root has the significance (Hebrew and Greek) 'to be fat'. In type it no doubt sets forth the holy energy which marked our Lord which knew but one object and which rebuked half-hearted loyalty or pretence. The Pharisee and the Herodian found the Divine energy which pierced their shallow minds and hypocritical hearts far too pungent and repulsive to their slothful pride. Their state of soul was disclosed by the unworldliness of One Who never had a thought but His Father's will, never took an interest in the world apart from God, and never came down to the level of ordinary men who had no place for God in their plans.

*Frankincense* (Hebrew *'lebonah'*; Greek *'libanos'*), from a root 'to be white', is of frequent occurrence in Scripture. It is a white gum and burns with a white flame. The English word 'frank' refers to its free burning quality. It speaks of the excellent purity and burning zeal which found its expression in Christ, in absolute consecration to God. No sentiment had place in His words. In the anticipation of sufferings which death would involve, He was consumed with a holy zeal for the glory and will of God, and all ascended to God as an offering of sweet-smelling savour. It was the burning frankincense which brought out the savour of the other sweet spices. Those three spices speak of that in our Lord's life which was hidden and for God's eye; whilst the four principal spices of the ointment tell of that which is external and carry the beauties of Christ into the world in witness to men. The incense expresses the graces of Christ, with the additional thought in the frankincense that they were brought out by the action of fire, that His exposure to the holy judgment of God on the Cross, when made sin, did but bring out all that was most precious and fragrant to God.

## The Ark

The Ark of the Covenant {Exodus 25:10-22} was the throne where God manifested Himself in the midst of Israel; it was also the seat of His sovereignty over every living man, as the God of the whole earth; and the expression also of relationship with His people. It was at the same time the setting forth of the Person of Christ and of His mediatorship between God and man. This latter is seen in the materials which composed it (acacia wood covered with gold, corresponding to the table and incense altar), in that which it contained, and in its dimensions. It was 2½ cubits in length and 1½ cubits in breadth and height. Reckoning in half cubits, 3 and 5: Divine and human, God and man, Immanuel, God with us. (In the brazen altar, the same number in cubits.) It will be seen that the half cubit is emphasised in each direction, and if, as in other parts of the Tabernacle, the ½ cubit is significant of the cross where Messiah was cut off, it also, in the case of the Ark, reminds us how closely connected are the cross and the throne, suffering and reigning.[38]

The 2 cubits would remind us of God's witness to His Son, and the 1 cubit of His purpose concerning Him, to

38 In the Old Testament the coming of Christ is seen as one thing; His life is seen passing at once into His glorious reign (Isaiah 9:6-7, Isaiah 11:1-9, Isaiah 51:1-3). This latter passage was cut in half by our Lord (Luke 4:19). We now know the things concerning our Lord have been divided into two parts, separated by a very long interval, nevertheless God's seal is set upon Him, 3 half cubits.

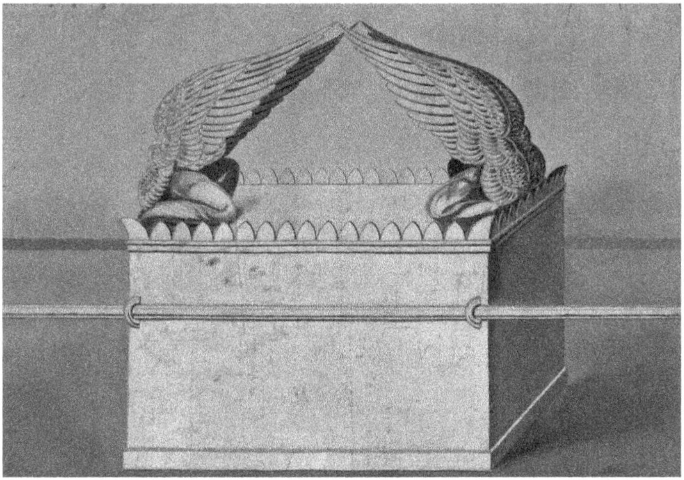

Figure 21: The Ark

be manifested in the day in which He shall be revealed, but known now by those who have liberty of access into the Holiest by the blood of Jesus.

In shape the Ark was a hollow chest or box, covered within and without with gold, the Divine nature of our Lord displayed over the form of a servant He had taken. All that God is was glorified by the Son of Man, and God has glorified Him in Himself.

The tables of the law were placed within the Ark, that is the second tables which Moses brought from the presence of God at Sinai. The sin of the golden calf made it impossible to bring the uncovered law into the midst of the people, for it would have condemned them to instant judgment.

On the second occasion of Moses' going up into the mount he was commanded of God to bring with him an Ark of wood, acacia wood, and therein was placed the re-written ten words of the law, the words "And they are there as Jehovah commanded me" {Deuteronomy 10:5,

J.N.D.} indicating that it was the same Ark, afterwards covered with gold, which was placed in the Holiest. The other articles comprising the furniture of the Tabernacle were remade or multiplied, but the Ark never was. It remained the abiding witness to God's purpose in Christ for Israel. He alone could say, "Thy law have I hid in my heart", and that law He magnified and made honourable. He laid down His life so perfect, bearing the curse of the law for those who had broken it, and took it out of the way as an instrument of condemnation for those who believe in Him, nailing it to His cross, His death being the witness of deliverance from it.

In Hebrews 9 the apostle speaks of the Ark having, besides the law, the golden pot that had manna and Aaron's rod that budded, though it is not certain as to whether these were placed within the Ark or beside it, probably the latter. Regarding the pot of manna, it is said, "Deposit it before Jehovah" (Exodus 16:33, J.N.D.), and in verse 34, "so Aaron deposited it before the Testimony". Of Aaron's rod that budded, "Jehovah said to Moses 'Bring Aaron's rod again before the Testimony to be kept as a token for the sons of rebellion'" (Numbers 17:10). So, as both the manna (Exodus 16:32) and the rod were to be seen, they could hardly have been within the Ark into which no man might look. The manna is typical of Christ in His lowly pathway here on earth, the rod speaks of the Priestly office to which He is called as risen from the dead.

Around the top of the Ark was a crown of gold. Hebrews 2:9 provides us with the significance of this, "We see Jesus Who was made a little lower than the angels for the suffering of death, crowned with glory and honour". Within this crown, of the same length and breadth as the Ark itself, there was a lid of pure gold forming the *mercy seat* upon which the Divine Presence or '*Shekinah*' was manifested. It was the place of meeting between Jehovah and Moses, it was the throne from whence commandment was given to the children of Israel (Exodus 25:22).

The mercy seat was of pure gold, typical of the intrinsic righteousness of God according to His own nature, what He ever is and ever will be, and that not only in the judgment of that which is contrary to Himself — of this the copper speaks. That which made the gold top a mercy seat was that upon it the blood was once sprinkled. Seven times it was sprinkled before it in the dust which, speaking of man's condition, provided his only standing in the presence of the glory of God, but only once upon the throne, for by one offering every attribute of God has been brought into harmonious working on behalf of man; lovingkindness and truth meeting together; righteousness and peace kissing each other (Psalm 85:10).

This is beautifully expressed in the cherubim upon the two ends of the mercy seat, beaten out of the same piece of gold. "Justice and judgment are the habitation of Thy throne" (Psalm 89:14). The faces of the cherubim were towards each other and towards the mercy seat (Exodus 25:20, 37:9). The cherubim represent the executors of the judgments of God. They are found at the gate of the garden of Eden forbidding all approach to the Tree of Life; upon the Ark they are looking upon the blood upon the gold; in the temple of Solomon they are looking outwards; and in Ezekiel 1, etc. they are seen as the supporters of the throne; and lastly in Revelation 4 as ascribing with the redeemed hosts, 'Glory to the Lamb'. The meaning of the name '*cherub*' is said to be derived from *ch* = 'as if' and *rub* = 'contending', 'as if contending' or demanding the judgment that sin deserves, all contention for this ceasing in presence of the blood which has met the judgment and brought it into 'one piece' with the love and mercy of God. No thickness is specified for the mercy seat, for who could measure "the depth of the riches both of the wisdom and knowledge of God! How unsearchable are His judgments, and His ways past finding out!" (Romans 11:33).

The covering wings speak of protecting power of heavenly grace. The executors of God's justice shelter all whom the blood has cleansed. Even the word used for the mercy seat *'kapporeth'* signifies a covering, the root word of which is *'kaphar'*, always used in connection with atonement, meaning a covering. The Septuagint translates *'kapporeth'* by *'hilasterion'* = propitiatory, and in Hebrews 9:5 the Holy Spirit uses this word, and again in Romans 3:25 applies it to our Lord Himself, 'set forth to be a propitiatory through faith in His blood'.

It is God's aspect towards all men that because of the blood upon the throne He can extend forgiveness to all who will draw near to Him on that ground. The mercy seat was no larger and no smaller than the Ark. Christ is sufficient in saving mercy, but there is nothing larger than He, the one and only way, the only Name by which man can be saved. All others are of no avail — no larger hope, no wider door. Again, the mercy seat was not smaller, for there is no such idea as man's works being needed to add to the sufficiency of the atoning work. "Not by works of righteousness which we have done, but according to His mercy He saved us" {Titus 3:5}. Not of works indeed, lest any man should boast and thus detract from the peerless work of the Christ of God.

Four rings of gold from which the staves were not to be taken, tell of the love unchanging which is the portion of His own, until the wilderness shall end and the rest of God has come. Then shall the cherubim look outward upon the fulfilment in blessing of His will by the Man of His good pleasure. Then shall the size of the golden cherubim of olive wood set forth the glory, the magnitude, the far-reaching glory of the work done at the Cross as compared with all else. But the Ark of acacia and gold shall be beneath all the glory, an eternal witness to Him Who was rich, but for our sakes became poor (1 Kings 6:23-28 and 8:3-8).

Judaism is distinguished from all other religions on earth by the fact of its ritual being prophetic and anticipatory, founded on the future and not on history, whereas all other religious systems are commemorative and historical. In Christianity both are combined. 'Ye do show the Lord's death', this is commemorative; 'Until He come', this is prophetic.

Two instances of irreverence in connection with the Ark are written for our learning. The first (2 Samuel 6.1-8). shows the jealousness of God in respect of the person of His Son. To add to, or depart from, the word of God as to this is to come under His chastening. The history of David before the Ark conveys a serious admonition. David before the Ark was acting contrary to the express direction of God as to the manner in which the ark should be carried, this giving occasion to the act of irreverence on the part of Uzziah in touching the Ark, which involved him in instant judgment. When men with the best of intentions substitute their own methods of carrying on the work of God, they must necessarily sustain it by human means. The doing so touches the majesty and glory of God concerning His Son into

Whose hands He has committed all authority and direction.

The second case is that of the men of Bethshemesh {1 Samuel 6}, who removed the mercy seat with the blood upon it, in order to look within, and in so doing came into the presence of the uncovered law, and in the consequent judgment 50,070 men perished. There is a serious warning in this for those who, ignoring the mercy of God which is only bestowed through the blood of Christ, are so irreverent as to attempt to stand before the holiness of God, in presence of the law, forgetful of His Divine Majesty and the only way of approach to Him Whose throne is established in Christ.

The cherubims of glory covering the mercy seat will have a future import in the return of the visible presence of Jehovah in the midst of Israel (Hebrews 9:5, Psalm 80:1). In four other passages is the phrase 'He dwelleth between the cherubims' used expressive of judgment, security and rest: 1 Samuel 4:4, 2 Kings 19:15, 1 Chronicles 13:6, Isaiah 37:16.

Four rings of gold, the symbol of Divine love were provided, for the Father loveth the Son and hath given all things into His hand. It is particularly specified that two rings were to be on one side and two on the other (Exodus 25:12), not on the corners under the border as in the case of the table; nor on the angles or ribs as the altar of incense; but on the sides, telling of the Father's love which it is our holy privilege to have part in with the Son (John 16:27, 17:23).

The coverings of the Ark were distinctive. Regarding the other vessels the badger skins were always outside but as to the Ark, it was the blue that was exterior. Firstly the vail was taken down and with this the ark and cherubim were covered. This laid particular emphasis upon the person of our Lord and showed how that the vail, that is to say His flesh, had not in anywise made less the glory of Him who is above all, God, blessed for ever.

The next covering of badger skins indicates how jealously this must be guarded with holy reverence. In taking upon Him the form of a servant there was no limitation of the attributes belonging to Godhead. That which He was in the beginning, He ever was and will be, although abiding a Man for ever.

These are holy mysteries, for the Father only knoweth the Son, but in the marvel of grace the Son has revealed the Father, hence the blue, so typical of that which belongs to heaven, was seen outside.

In the different vessels, the blue, though beneath, has different connections (Numbers 4). The instruments of the lampstand were *under* the blue (verse 9), those of the table were *upon* the blue (verse 7), and those belonging to the altar of incense were put separately *in* a cloth of blue (verse 12). The first speaks of character, the second of presentation, the third of communion; the whole emphasizes "That as is the heavenly One so are the heavenly ones" (1 Corinthians 15{:48}).

The word '*Shekinah*' is so often used in relation to the Divine Presence in the pillars of cloud and fire, and manifested between the cherubim, that it is well to notice that the word nowhere occurs in the Old Testament. It is a derivative of a Hebrew root signifying 'to dwell'. In Jewish writings subsequent to the Bible it is used as expressive of the presence of God manifested in the burning bush, the pillar of cloud, etc.. Thus in Numbers 5:3, "In the midst whereof I dwell" is rendered by the Targum "Among whom my *shekinah* is dwelling".

Jewish authorities speak of the *shekinah* upon the mercy seat, and hold that it did not return to the second temple. The following Scriptures are decisive as to a visible presence in the Holiest of the Tabernacle: Exodus 25:22, 29:42, 30:6, 33:11; Leviticus 16:2; Numbers 17:4, 12:7-8.

On the return of the remnant of Jews from Babylon to Jerusalem the altar was restored and the temple rebuilt, but there is no mention of the Ark and consequently no manifested presence; this was because they as a nation were still *'Lo-ammi'* {not My people} and sovereignty was not to be restored to them. Nor will it be until they shall confess Him Whom they have despised and rejected, to be both Lord and Christ. Then shall the glory again be upon earth and the prophecies of Ezekiel 43:2-9 and Haggai 2:7-9 be fulfilled by the presence of Him Who is King of Kings and Lord of Lords.

Ezekiel speaks only of the two altars in his vision of the millennial temple; no Ark, because Christ, Whom it typified, will be present; no Lampstand, because the Spirit will be poured out upon all flesh; no Table, because the purpose of God for Israel will be fulfilled. The remembrance of the sacrificial work and the consequent worship will abide. See Jeremiah 3:16-18.

The last mention of the Ark[39] is in the days of Josiah (2 Chronicles 35:3), and Jeremiah's word to them at that time was that they should no longer have it as an object before them; for they had come to regard it with the superstitious ideas they accorded to their idols. In the days to come when Israel shall be restored to their land, they shall not say, "The Ark of the Covenant of the Lord; neither shall it come to mind; neither shall they

[39] See Appendix 1: *The History of the Ark.*

remember it; neither shall they visit it; neither shall it be magnified any more." The Name of the Lord shall take the place of the Ark as God's gathering centre for all nations (Isaiah 2:1-5, Micah 4:1-5).

It is significant that when the Tabernacle is set up (Exodus 40) no mention is made of sprinkling with blood, which was undoubtedly done (see Hebrews 9:21) upon the Tabernacle and its vessels; upon Aaron and his sons, only the anointing oil is referred to. The reason seems to be, that whatever sin on our part might call for, we have here the whole scene of creation, all things in heaven and all things on earth, claimed in the power of the Spirit (the oil) in virtue of Christ's Person and Title; just as He was in fact anointed with the Holy Spirit and with power, apart from blood-shedding.

## Chapter 19:
## The Robes of the High Priest

— holy garments for glory and for beauty. Perhaps of all the things that are patterns of things in the heavens, none bring so near to us the Person of Christ in the present exercise of the office of priest as the consideration of these articles of attire; for if we are to profit by His priestly service on our behalf, it must involve a close personal acquaintance with Him, and the bringing of all to Him without reserve. There must also be submission to the searching of the Word of God. It is with these two things that in the epistle to the Hebrews the Priesthood of our Lord is introduced (chapter 4:12-13). Then seeing that we have such a great High Priest, glorious in Person, the Son; high in position, in the heavens; One Who perfectly understands us and all that tries and tests us, for He had full experience of the same, we may be assured that in all things He will provide seasonable help. As our Advocate, He lifts us when we fall, but as Priest He can keep us from falling. But this is not the whole object for which our Lord fills the priestly office. Necessary as it is to provide the grace for trial, infirmity and ignorance, the end before Him is to lead us as worshippers of the Father into the Holiest of all.

None but One so great, Who is made higher than the heavens, could avail for this. The revolt from Rome and her priestcraft, which ever permeates Protestantism in a more or less diluted form, has resulted in Christians losing the truth of the very urgent need of a priest if we are to be carried in triumph through the wilderness, and be worshippers of the Father in spirit and in truth.

Clearly no priest of the Aaronic order could suffice for this, much less any who have no qualification but that which is derived from man. So great, so exalted is the Christian privilege to enter the Holiest that a priest is needed who is holy, guileless, undefiled, separated from sinners and become higher than the heavens, One Who has completely disposed of the question of sin on account of those He represents, and further, Who has been unchangeably constituted priest by the oath of God.

Such an One is Jesus, the Son of God, a priest for ever after the order of Melchisedek. Hebrews 8:4 shows that the priesthood after this order does not belong to earth, for when on earth our Lord came of the tribe of Judah, of which tribe Moses spake nothing concerning priesthood. Also, as the Order of Melchisedek is for ever, it is evident that all question of death must be eliminated for it to abide in the power of endless life.

The priests of Aaron's order never finished their work and were unable by the offering of the blood of bulls and goats to take away sins, and in consequence rend the vail. On account of this, no seats were provided in the Tabernacle, the priests who officiated therein never sat down. But Christ takes up His priestly service when, all sacrifice for sin having been completed, He sits down in heaven itself at the right hand of God. Like Melchisedek,

He is occupied with blessing those who come unto God by Him with the joy of God, and bringing to God the joy of the appreciation of Himself in the hearts of His children, the priestly family He represents. This is the characteristic of the Melchisedek Order, it was concerned only with blessing and not with offering for sin.

The garments which Aaron wore are typical of a higher order of priesthood than he could fill, and never in those garments could he enter the Holiest of all. It is also significant that the robes were typical of a higher order, that they were not re-made, but the son that was priest in his father's stead put them on for seven days at his consecration. The robes set forth One Who, continuing ever, has an unchangeable priesthood (Exodus 29:29-30; compare Hebrews 7:23-24).

The *sons of Aaron* were typical of the priestly family including all believers. Under the law they formed a special class, but in Christianity there is no such thing: all saints take character from association with Christ; all are made kings and priests to His God and Father; all constitute a holy priesthood to offer up spiritual sacrifices; all are a royal priesthood to show forth the praises of Him Who hath called us out of darkness into His marvellous light.

We have before noted that the number nine does not occur in the Tabernacle measurements because as it represents the oath of God, it could not be attached to a passing order. It is significant however that the priestly garments with which Aaron was attired were nine in number, and the name Melchisedek occurs just nine times in the Epistle to the Hebrews.

It is necessary to read both Exodus 28 and 39, to obtain a list of all the holy garments. For instance, the linen breeches are described in Exodus 28:42-43, but only alluded to in Exodus 39:28. So also the inner girdle is described in Exodus 39:29, and only just mentioned in Exodus 28:39. Again the phrase 'To minister unto Me' occurs four times in Exodus 28, but not in Exodus 39. Instead 'As the Lord commanded Moses' occurs seven times in Exodus 39, but not in Exodus 28. It will be noticed in Exodus 28, that three times 'That he may minister unto Me in the priest's office' is said of Aaron (verses 1, 3, 4), and once when Aaron's sons are associated with him, in verse 41, 'That they may minister'.

Between verses 4 and 41 of Exodus 28, the nine priestly garments are specified, the linen breeches not being included but described separately, in verses 42 and 43. The linen of the breeches was of the same kind as the linen garments of the High Priest when he entered the Holiest with the blood of the sin-offering. These garments were necessary because the wearing of them made Aaron and his sons *typically* what Christ is *personally*. They were sinners, He was and is the sinless One, a Minister of the Sanctuary which the Lord has pitched and not man.

The nine articles of priestly attire which Aaron wore were:–

1. The embroidered linen coat.
2. The inner girdle.
3. The blue robe of the ephod.
4. The ephod.
5. The curious girdle of the ephod.
6. The onyx stones.

7. The breastplate.
8. The holy plate.
9. The mitre.

Each of these is descriptive of some characteristic of the priesthood of our Lord, each reflects some ray of the glory and honour with which He is crowned.

### THE EMBROIDERED LINEN COAT

In the Tabernacle types three kinds of linen were employed.

(a) The fine twined linen of which the curtains of the court and the fabrics of the tabernacle were composed, representing the perfect righteousness which marked our Lord's pathway through the world. So perfect was this that none could answer His challenge, "Which of you convinceth me of sin?" {John 8:46}.

(b) The straight or shining linen of which the garments of Aaron were made when on the great Day of Atonement he entered into the Holiest (Leviticus 16:4). Holiness was characteristic of these, and they signify the holy nature and intrinsic purity necessary in One Who makes atonement for others: "He who knew no sin"; "Who did no sin"; "In Him is no sin" {2 Corinthians 5:21, 1 Peter 2:22, 1 John 3:5}.

(c) The *embroidered* coat of damask linen placed beneath Aaron's other garments (Exodus 28:4, 39; 39:27). This is typical of the graces of our Lord Jesus which were embroidered upon all His words and deeds, the way, indeed, in which He did things and which made Him so attractive. "They wondered at the gracious words which proceeded out of His mouth" {Luke 4:22}. How tender His compassion, how gentle, how kind. In every act, He, the Holy and Beloved of

God, exhibited to erring and sinful men and women bowels of mercies, kindness, humbleness of mind, meekness, longsuffering, forbearance and forgiveness. Unchanged in His present glory, this is the moral beauty upon which His priesthood rests.

Figure 22: The High Priest on the Day of Atonement

He is *a gracious Priest*, One to Whom we can tell the deep secrets of the heart, assured of His tenderest sympathy with our sorrows, taking our infirmities and bearing our sicknesses as He ever did, sharing our tears at the same time that He gives us to know that He is the Resurrection and the Life. "For we have not an High Priest Who cannot sympathise (literal translation) with our weaknesses" {Hebrews 4:15}.

There is but one word in Greek to express 'weakness' and 'infirmity' (*ἀσθένεια*, *'astheneia'*). "In all points tempted like as we are, without sin" {Hebrews 4:15}. This last clause excludes that which is sinful, for no Christian desires the Lord's sympathy with the sinful nature he finds in himself, it is the Lord's death which meets this. But there is not a detail of our weakness, under every form of trial and testing, that Jesus our great High Priest upon the Throne of God does not enter into in the perfect sympathy of a human heart, and with all the Divine strength of His compassion. So the Throne where He sits becomes a throne of grace, where all who come to Him may find for every phase of need, seasonable help.

Weakness is not sinful, Christ was crucified in weakness, (same word, *'astheneia'*) {2 Corinthians 13:4}. Christ's strength is made perfect in weakness, and Paul gloried in it that the power of Christ may rest upon him {2 Corinthians 12:9}. Suffering is not sinning, but it is just in the weakness and suffering that the unceasing ministry of our Divine Priest provides the resources of Divine grace that He so fully proved. "Father, not My will but Thine be done" {Luke 22:42}. Happy indeed the soul that rises far beyond the thought of resignation into the consciousness that whatsoever the Father's will is must be best. It is thus that our Lord's priestly intercession and grace ministers to us grace and strength to support His own dependent life in us, which is yet in earthen vessels. The exercise of His priesthood never ceases for all saints. He ever lives to intercede for us, continually He thinks of and cares for us. This will, however, lead us on, not only in the knowledge of the character of our Lord's priesthood expressed in the linen robe, but to see the personal application of it in His girding with the girdle.

## The Inner Girdle

The inner girdle (''*abnet*') alluded to in Exodus 28:39, and described in Exodus 39:29, was of needlework of fine twined linen, blue, purple and scarlet, but no gold. It must not be confused with the curious girdle of the ephod, in which gold was present and which was of cunning work. This inner girdle, unseen when Aaron was robed, is expressive of *a serving priest*, and such our Lord is. We may well wonder that amidst the hosts of the redeemed and the serried ranks of angelic powers, He has individual care and thought for each of His sheep, and the feeblest too, a care and service that is known only to him who receives it. In John 13 He is girded with the towel, to comfort those whose feet He washes from the soils of earth; in Revelation 1 He is girded at the breasts with a golden girdle, not the restraining of affection as some have thought, but the service of His love for those who love Him, to make them overcomers in Divine righteousness amid the corruption with which His witness on earth is marred.

Yet again it shall be His joy in glory to serve, for it is love's delight so to do, for He will for His watching servants gird Himself and make them to sit down to meat and come forth and serve them (Luke 12{:37}).

There is nothing that makes the Lord so personally real to the soul as this secret service of His love, and it is this which is so essential if the further unfolding of His priestly office is to be apprehended.

How necessary, if we are to enter into all that He is as Minister of the Sanctuary, that He should first sup with us, so that in the intimacy of His presence the heart may unburden itself, tell to Him the secret trials to which no other ear may listen, and in doing so find the burden lifted by His sympathy and compassion that so fully understands our infirmity.

This girdle was composed of fine linen, blue, purple and scarlet, and this, too, enhances the wonder that One so great and glorious should condescend to our littleness, and come not as a visitor but to abide, until the night, already far spent, shall end in the revelation of Him so long known in grace.

> No fleeting glance is mine, no passing word.
> Thou dwellst, as once with Thy disciples, Lord—
> Never upbraiding, condescending, free,
> 'Tis thus I know, O Lord, Thou art with me![40]

This inner girdle, binding the embroidered coat of the graces displayed in the wilderness path He trod, tells to the heart that the throne which is now His has made no difference to the tender care of love for the feeblest of His sheep, and that each of these may know:–

> The sweet companionship of One
> Who once the desert trod;
> The glorious fellowship with One
> Upon the throne of God;

40 {Adapted from original 3rd verse of "Abide with me" by H. F. Lyte (1793-1847)}

The joy no desolations here
Can reach, or cloud, or dim—
The present Lord, the living God,
And we *alone* with Him.[41]

## The Blue Robe of the Ephod

The robe of blue {Exodus 28:4, 31-32; 39:22-23}, called the robe of the ephod because before that garment of priestly service in its highest character can be understood, that which lies beneath it must be known. This robe reached from the neck to the feet, its colour being symbolic of heavenly love, and presents the service of our Lord in the character of *a loving Priest*. It is with the love of God, the love of the Father, that our great High Priest desires to impress us. A love whose only measure is that wherewith the Son is loved; the character of which is in the relationship which belongs to the Son; the intimacy of which is expressed by the Son in the words, "Thou lovest them as Thou lovest Me" {John 17:23}. It is the Son Who is a priest for ever after the order of Melchisedek, and as such He ministers, to all who come unto God through Him, the fulness of the love which called forth from His heart worship to His God and Father. Where such love is known, worship must follow, and without it no true worship can be.

The opening at the collar of this robe was a hole made like to an habergeon or coat of mail, and so strongly was this woven that it was not possible to rend it. How confirmatory is this of the love of God in Christ Jesus our Lord, from which neither death nor life, nor angels nor principalities, nor powers, nor things present, nor things to come, nor height, nor depth, nor any other creature can separate us. It is this love which the present

41 {(P.B.) Mrs E. F. Bevan (1827-1909)}

Figure 23: The Robes of the High Priest

activity of the priesthood of Christ ministers to us. This love is the bond of unity (Psalm 133), like the precious ointment that was on the head of Aaron, that ran down upon his beard, and went down to the skirts of his garments.

Upon the hem of the robe of blue there were bells and pomegranates arranged alternately (Exodus 28:33-34; {39:25-26}), the object of the bells being that when Aaron was within the Holy, out of sight, the sound heard without was proof to those who listened that Aaron was living. Thus although our Lord is at present unseen, carrying on His ministry in the heavenly sanctuary, two proofs are afforded of this fact. One is the continuance of the Gospel testimony, and the other is that fruit is in evidence in those who believe, represented by the pomegranates. These were made of blue, purple and scarlet, twined; for the saints now stand in all the acceptance of Christ, but no fine linen is mentioned (Exodus 28:33; 39:24). This would seem to show that the day for the display of the righteousnesses of the saints is not yet (Revelation 19:8), but belongs to the hour of Christ's appearing, "When He shall appear we shall be like Him" (1 John 3:2).

## The Ephod

The ephod {Exodus 28:4-6; 39:2-4}, which partly covered the robe of blue (for that which speaks of the love of God must ever be in mind however great the glory displayed upon it), was made of gold, blue, purple, scarlet and fine twined linen. It represents our adorable Lord as *a great or glorious Priest*. The witness of the Divine is seen in the gold, spoken of first to give prominence to it. All the other materials were interwoven with this, for which purpose it was beaten into thin plates and cut into wires and so wrought that it could not be separated without destroying the whole fabric.

This is one of the holiest mysteries of our faith, the interweaving of the Divine and human which the

Gospel presents to us. Now ascended on high, He has not laid aside the human, but perfect Man and God over all blessed for ever, He abides a Priest continually. The glories of Sonship shine forth in Him, in His acceptance we enter the Divine Presence to worship as sons before the Father.

The ephod consisted of a front and back portion united on the shoulders, and open at the sides, so that the robe of blue was everywhere seen. 'Love Divine our present portion, Heaven's choicest store.'[42] There were no cherubim embroidered in the ephod, for no question of judgment enters into the service of our great High Priest after the order of Melchisedek, the sacrifice has been offered, the victory won, and only the blessing of those He brings to God, and the worship the Father seeks, is His occupation now.

The ephod was characteristically the priestly garment and to it were attached the curious girdle, the breastplate and the onyx shoulder stones.

We have said that the ephod represents Christ as a glorious or great High Priest, and in it we may see the Father's thoughts of the Son. As John expresses it, "Our fellowship is with the Father" {1 John 1:3}. How supremely wonderful it is to be in the hands of so great a Priest, One on Whom the Father's delight rests and Whom He has glorified in Himself, and what joy to the Son to minister to us the love which "rests on Him in those bright courts above".[43]

The ephod was of cunning work, both sides alike. No superficial glory such as men glory in, but intrinsic excellence and personal worth. Let us then consider the

42 Inglis Fleming (1859-1955)

43 James Boyd (1851-1936)

High Priest of our confession, Christ Jesus, and as was said of Melchisedek, "Consider how great this man was" {Hebrews 7:4}.

### THE CURIOUS GIRDLE OF THE EPHOD

The ephod was bound to the person of Aaron by the curious girdle {Exodus 28:4, 8; 39:5}. This was of the same workmanship as the ephod and is so closely connected with it that in Exodus 29:5 'and gird him with the curious girdle of the ephod', and in Leviticus 8:7 'and bound it unto him therewith', the expression is literally 'and ephodized him with it'. The object apparently is to convey the thought of the intimate connection between the symbolic glories of the ephod and the person who wore it. The word translated 'curious girdle' is not that which is usually employed for a girdle (*ayzore*) but is a Hebrew word (*khaysheb*) meaning a curious device or embroidery, and is solely used to express this belt. Another word (*abneht*) is exclusively used for the inner, unseen girdle. The girdle of the ephod is expressive of our Lord as *a worshipping Priest*, responding to the Father's love and leading the worship of those the Father has given to Him by imparting to them His own thoughts of the Father. "*Our* fellowship is with His Son Jesus Christ" {1 John 1:3}.

The ephod and the girdle are thus united: the ephod being the manifestation of the Son to him with whom He sups; the girdle, the abode of the Father and the Son revealed to those who sup with Him. The ephod and girdle resemble the curtains and vail, except that the two last had no gold, and the first two no cherubim. In the door and the gate there was neither gold nor cherubim.

The materials which we have seen typify the glories of Christ are also connected with the various aspects of the sacrifices offered upon the altar, namely:

| | |
|---|---|
| *The gold* | The Divine excellence of the Person offered up, which makes the offering of eternal efficacy. |
| *The blue* | The burnt offering of Him Who came from heaven, presented wholly to God. |
| *The purple* | The peace offering on the ground of which He, the Prince of Peace, shall reign. |
| *The scarlet* | The sin offering, necessary if others redeemed by blood are to have part with Him in His reign (compare Psalm 149:9). |
| *The white linen* | The meat offering, indicating the spotless purity of Him Who, though made sin, knew no sin. |

All this beautifully harmonises with the glories that are to follow, when He shall be manifested as the Sent One of the Father, the universal Lord, the King upon David's throne and the Son of God's love, Heir of all things.

Two rings of gold were made and fastened to the fore part of the ephod {Exodus 39:20}, the word 'underneath' seeming to indicate that although they were above, or at the upper part of the girdle, they were hidden by it. Beautifully symbolic is this of the secret witness of the love of God upon which is fastened all His counsels for Israel and the Church, revealed to those who worship the Father in spirit and in truth. To these were attached laces of blue connected with similar rings upon the lower border of the breastplate inward, that is, hidden as were the other rings, the object being in connection with the other attachments absolute security: "That the breastplate might not be loosed from the ephod" {Exodus 39:21}. We may recall, in this connection 2 Corinthians 1:19-22, "Now He that stablisheth us with you in Christ", literally "attaches firmly to" or "connects firmly with".

Before considering the breastplate, the shoulder stones call for our attention, for unto these the breastplate was fastened by wreathen chains of gold, in which the symbol of power is easily read. Every saint is ever on the heart of Christ and held there by the power of Divine righteousness above and Divine love beneath.

### The Onyx Stones

The onyx stones upon the shoulders set in ouches of gold {Exodus 28:9-14; 39:6-7}, had engraved upon them the names of the twelve sons of Israel according to their birth.

| ***Right shoulder*** | | ***Left shoulder*** | |
|---|---|---|---|
| Reuben | Simeon | Gad | Asher |
| Levi | Judah | Issachar | Zebulon |
| Dan | Naphtali | Joseph | Benjamin |

This is deeply suggestive of the order connected with the new birth; for God's children are born in succession and put as such upon the shoulder of the great Shepherd of the sheep. The onyx also is a significant stone; in the breastplate the name of Asher was written upon it, the meaning of which is 'happy or joyful'. It is mentioned with the gold that was found in the land of Havilah {Genesis 2:11-12} (= circular or eternal), and bdellium (= separation). All this surely recalls Luke 15{:5}, 'He layeth it on His shoulders rejoicing'. Each believer is eternally separated to God for His own joy, in the power of Divine righteousness. The onyx stones with their chains of gold, strongly wreathed together set forth *a mighty Priest*; the two chains remind us of the hands of the Father and the Son from Whose clasp no adverse power can snatch the feeblest of the sheep.

## The Breastplate

The breastplate and its attachments could never be loosed from the ephod. The unchangeable priesthood of Christ is representative of all saints, He is *a representative Priest*. Made of the same materials and workmanship as the ephod, it was doubled so as to form a square measuring a span in length and breadth. The surface was filled with fillings of stones (see {Authorized Version} margin) entirely, so no room for anything else alongside the purpose of God for His people Israel. The still more unique purpose concerning the Church could not at that time be disclosed, but in the shadow we may read the substance, and see that which is dearer to the heart of Christ than ought {anything} else. Note the words twice repeated in Exodus 28:29-30, 'Upon his heart.'

The stones were set in fillings of gold, and thus every name was represented in righteousness Divine in the Holy, before Jehovah continually. These names were not according to their birthdays, but according to the twelve tribes, that is, the order in which God pleased to place them around Himself. God fits His saints together, puts them in relation to each other, according to the good pleasure of His will, that they may reflect and exhibit His glory. This shall be fully seen in the coming day both in Jerusalem on earth, and in the city of the living God, the heavenly Jerusalem.

Three lists of precious stones are given in Scripture:–

1. In Exodus 28{:17-20} they reflect the light of *grace*.
2. In Ezekiel 28:13 they reflect the light of *creation*.
3. In Revelation 21{:19-20} they reflect the light of *glory*.

These precious stones have no light in themselves, but are formed so as to break up the light that falls upon them, and exhibit God in relation to grace, creation and glory as the Father of lights.

### The Urim and Thummim

In the breastplate was put the Urim and Thummim = lights and perfections. (Septuagint: *delosis* and *aletheia* = manifestation and truth.) The plural form shows intensity. It is useless to try to materialise these, nor are we intended to do so. Both are found in Christ and it is His presence that makes His saints what they are, and gives them the discernment of His mind and will. For this reason the breastplate was known as the breastplate of judgment. All the light of the revelation of the moral character of God has shone forth and is in Christ; He is the effulgence of God's glory, this answers to the Urim. Again, He is the expression in perfection of the Divine Substance, the Image of the invisible God, God manifest, God seen and heard, this answers to the Thummim.

In the case of the Tabernacle there was no doubt a connection between the *Shekinah* on the ark and the Urim and Thummim in the breastplate, for this glory being wanting in the second temple, there was no Urim and Thummim available (Nehemiah 7:65), nor will there be on earth until of Levi it is said, 'Let thy Thummim and thy Urim be with thy holy One' (Deuteronomy 33:8).

### THE TWELVE JEWELS

There were four rows of stones:–

| | | | |
|---|---|---|---|
| The first row: | CARBUNCLE<br>Zebulon | TOPAZ<br>Issachar | SARDIUS<br>Judah |
| The second row: | DIAMOND<br>Gad | SAPPHIRE<br>Simeon | EMERALD<br>Reuben |
| The third row: | AMETHYST<br>Benjamin | AGATE<br>Manasseh | LIGURE<br>Ephraim |
| The fourth row: | JASPER<br>Naphtali | ONYX<br>Asher | BERYL<br>Dan |

What can we learn from these? Surely the Holy Spirit has some definite instruction regarding these jewels secured upon the ephod of Aaron.

In the first place the breastplate which rested on the heart of the High Priest is expressive of the worship which Christ as High Priest renders to God, and in which the redeemed are associated with Him. This worship consists in the presentation to God the Father of His own excellencies in Person and Work, in the presence of the glory of the throne, and in the value of the response of love from His own heart.

The breastplate is also typical of what the Church will be as the vessel of unending worship in heaven, to which Israel will correspond on earth. As Aaron stood at the golden altar offering the incense which spoke of the fragrance of Christ to God, although there was at that time a vail between, he did so in the presence of the glory upon the Ark, and also with the light of the intrinsic excellence within the breastplate, the Urim and Thummim, which exhibited through the jewels the typical glories attaching to the death, resurrection, ascension and coming of the Son of God.

Remembering that it is as the Man of Joy our Lord fulfils His priestly office, we may gather instruction not only from the names engraved on the stones but in reference to the man of happiness described in the Psalms. The word used in that book is *'asheri'* signifying 'happiness'. It is only used as an interjection and in the plural, and would be best rendered by "Oh! how happy is", or "Oh! the happinesses of", and expresses the joy belonging to the believer in association with Christ in Divine righteousness, for it must be observed that all the jewels are set in gold.

The first row of 3 stones is emblematic of *the results of the Cross.*

1. *Sardius* (*'odem'*), the same three letters of which compose the name 'Adam', and the last two letters of which are the name for blood — {*'dam'*}. The Sardius or ruby is the stone of redemption, on which the name of Judah = 'praise', is very suitably inscribed.

How great is the joy of our great High Priest in having finished the work which the Father had given Him to do. The Lion of the tribe of Judah is the Lamb that was slain, and upon this would the happinesses of the man of Psalm 84:4 depend. Christ has indeed passed through the valley of weeping, satisfied the altar's claim and now praises in the strength of Jehovah.

2. *Topaz* ({*'pitdah'*}), a stone of amber colour, which we may gather from Ezekiel 1:27 is symbolic of service,

downward and upward. On this stone was written the name of Issachar = 'hire or recompense'.

It speaks of Him Who for the joy that was set before Him, endured the Cross, despising the shame; and now in the happiness of Psalm 128:1-2, one of the songs of upgoings, He eats of the fruit of the labour of His hands, the recompense of the sore travail of His soul; and in that joy He now worships, saluted of God, a High Priest after the order of Melchisedek. The joy of rest after labour is connected with this stone.

3. *Carbuncle* ({*'barequeth'*}). This is also a red stone, a remembrance of the redemption work which the ruby set forth. On this was engraved the name of Zebulon = 'dwelling or restful abiding'.

The work is fully accomplished and the Workman has sat down, for in connection with the priesthood of Christ there is no sacrificial service. That has been done and needs no addition. His office as priest is engaged in blessing God and filling those who come to God by Him with fulness of joy. His is the happiness of the Man of God's choice, and in Him we too may approach to dwell in His courts, to be satisfied with the goodness of His house, even of His holy temple (Psalm 65:4).

Thus do the jewels of the first row speak of the present joy of Christ and of the priestly service by which He imparts His joy to our hearts, in order that we may join the praises that He leadeth.

The second row, emerald, sapphire and diamond, have in them the thought of personality and are connected with *the joy that belongs to resurrection.*

4. *Emerald* ({*'nophek'*}), a vivid green stone; the ancients esteemed the sight of it to be a cure for sore eyes.

Inscribed upon it was the name Reuben = 'see a son', which makes the prevailing thought that of 'sonship', corresponding to the happiness of Psalm 2:7, 12.

Certain it is that the spiritual vision is only rightly adjusted when it rests upon the glory of the beloved Son of God. The joy of worship is this that it takes character from the relationship in which the Son stands to the Father, for in the eternal circle of love Divine is the sweetest refreshment and the deepest joy. In the light of unsullied glory He bears the names of "The Beloved", "The Son of His love".

Millennial majesty shall make known to the universe that the Father loves the Son, and the joyous worship of the ages shall express the response of the Son to the unique affection which was His before all worlds. The rainbow of Revelation 4, wholly emerald, is emblematic of the joy of the Son glorified again in the Father. This aspect of the priesthood is very precious, for it shows the greatness of the Person by whom we have boldness to enter the holiest of the Father's presence, accepted in the Beloved.

5. *Sapphire* ({*'sappir'*}). The meaning of this stone we have already become acquainted with.[44] It is of pure deep blue colour and bore upon it the name of Simeon = 'hearing', which very suitably answers to the sapphire = 'declaration'.

It typifies the joy of our Lord on the resurrection morning in declaring the Name of the Father in the ears of those whom He could salute as His brethren, "I ascend to My Father and your Father; to My God and your God" {John 20:17}. Its colour is symbolic of the depths of heavenly love into which these words

44 Chapter 3: Preceding Circumstances, page 30.

introduce us. The name of Levi = 'joined', does not occur in the breastplate, but in the words which Jacob spoke to his sons. Simeon and Levi are associated, so also is 'hearing' and 'joining', pointing to the joy of our great High Priest in joining those who hear His message in the supreme relationship belonging to Himself (compare Psalm 119:1-2).

6. *Diamond, or Sardonyx* (R.V.) ({'*yahalom*'}). The Diamond corresponding to the Jasper which is the last stone of the series. The Sardonyx was a reddish stone with brown and white bands. Upon it was the name of Gad = 'a troop'.

It symbolizes the joy of our Lord in presenting to the Father the many sons of His purpose gathered by the previous declaration. The varied bands of colour are suggestive of gathering together in one the children of God scattered abroad, and the joy exceeding with which He will present them in the presence of His glory (Jude 24). As this stone stands in relation to Israel, it speaks of the gathering together of the rod of His inheritance by which every opposing force arrayed against His purpose will be broken to pieces. See Jeremiah 51:19-23. This will be when Priesthood shall be joined to Kingship (Zechariah 6:13), and in answer to the request of the Son that shall then be made (Psalm 2:8), the uttermost parts of the earth shall be given Him.

The third row is suggestive of *joy connected with ascension*: ligure, agate and amethyst.

7. *Ligure, or Jacinth* (R.V.). This has in the Hebrew ({'*leshem*'}) a dual termination indicative of double fruit or increase, and suitably the name of Ephraim = 'fruitful', is upon it. As that name stands in place of Joseph it is easy to see that it expresses figuratively the

joy of exaltation from the lowest to the highest, and of the fruitfulness that shall abound to the man of Psalm 1:1-3.

Ascension is the earnest of the abounding increase that shall redound to the glory of God, when the Son shall see of the fruit and travail of His soul and shall be satisfied. The sweet anticipation of that joy lends its own character to the present worship of our great High Priest.

8. *Agate*. The Hebrew word (*'sheb-oo'*) only occurs in Exodus 28:19 and 39:12. It is derived from a root meaning 'transport' or 'carry away' and written on it was the name of Manasseh = 'forgetfulness'. This is very characteristic of the joy of the man of Psalm 32:1-2, but much more so of the transport of happiness which shall obliterate all sorrow, wipe away all tears and dismiss death and sighing and crying into complete forgetfulness. The former things shall not be remembered or come into mind (Isaiah 65:17).

The worship of our great High Priest leads us even now into the new creation's fadeless joy. In the presence of Him Who is the beginning of the Creation of God, old things have passed away, behold all things are become new. The agate has the sense of detachment as illustrated by Psalm 45:10-11. "Hearken, O daughter, and consider, and incline thine ear; forget also thine own people, and thy father's house. So shall the King greatly desire thy beauty; for He is thy Lord; and worship thou Him." Worship is marked by singleness of eye, its outlook is upward and forward, it is absorbed with the excellent greatness of its object and the things of the Divine purpose made known in the Son.

9. *Amethyst* ({*'achlamah'*}), a stone of a fine violet or purple colour, bearing on it the name of Benjamin = 'Son of my right hand'. How full is all this of the thought of supremacy. The one who was Benoni, son of his mother's sorrow, is now seen as reigning a priest upon His throne.

The joy of Christ will be to administer all things to the glory of God in order that in final result He may hand back the kingdom to God, even the Father, that God may be all in all. In view of the happiness with which He shall fill this sorrow stricken earth, the Psalmist may well exclaim, "Happy is that people that is in such a case, yea happy is that people whose God is the Lord" (Psalm 144:15). To this all heaven shall respond (Revelation 5.12), until not only heaven and earth, but the infernal regions, with all that are in the sea shall ascribe "Blessing and honour and glory and power be unto Him that sitteth upon the throne and unto the Lamb for ever and ever" (Revelation 5:13; compare Philippians 2:9-11).

The fourth row beryl, onyx, jasper, is connected with *manifestation.*

10. *Beryl*[45]. The Hebrew word is *'tarshish'* meaning 'to break, subdue'. On this stone was engraved the name of Dan = 'judge', and it stands connected with the exhibition of Divine judgment in the hands of the Son of Man (John 5:22, 27). Daniel ('God is my judge')

45 J.N.D. and F.W.Grant both read 'chrysolite', R.V. 'beryl' with 'chalcedony' in margin. The symbolism of chrysolite and beryl are similar. The former is from *'chrysos'* – *'gold'* – and *'lithos'* a stone, both of which suggest Divine righteousness and judgment. In the cross these find their fullest expression. It is also the joy of the bride in Song of Solomon 5:14 to see the hands of her beloved as gold rings set with the chrysolite = the beryl. She is the work of those hands, the fruit of that endless love which has made her His own.

records in his 10th chapter how he saw a certain man in his vision whose body was like the beryl, who had authority over kingdoms. Ezekiel also saw the beryl in connection with the wheels of God's government (Ezekiel 1:16).

All worship must emphasize the will and judgement of God to Whom it is addressed, and in this lies our sure anchor ground, our fortress hill, if indeed we have learned from our great High Priest the secret that the will of God is equivalent to fulness of joy, and when that will is done on earth as it is in heaven, then a universe of bliss will ensue. The consciousness of this caused David to exclaim, "O how blessed, how happy are they that keep judgment and he that doeth righteousness at all times" (Psalm 106:3). It was the knowledge that all things shall be adjusted according to the good pleasure of the will of God that gave to Paul the note of worship in Ephesians 1{:3}, "Blessed be the God and Father of our Lord Jesus Christ".

11. *Onyx* ({*'shoham'*}). The Septuagint reads (*βηρύλλιον*) instead of 'onyx'. We learn from Job 28:16 that this was a very precious stone. Its Hebrew name means 'to shine with the lustre of fire' and on it was written the name Asher = 'happy'.

It clearly sets forth the greatness of the joy of Him Who is anointed with the oil of gladness above His fellows. We have seen, too, how the stones upon the shoulders of the High Priest, which were likewise onyx, express the joy of the Shepherd Who finds the sheep, so that we are not surprised that it is stated to be very precious and truly so in His eyes. Worship which flows from this joy becomes for the servant, as it was for the Master, the strength and energy of true service. Such service is not from the demand of a legal obedience, but is the response of love, which like a vehement flame, needs no urging. Its energy is found in the knowledge of God, and as the Psalmist said, in the happiness of having the God of Jacob for help, and the Lord God for hope (Psalm 146:5).

To Asher belongs the special portion, the fat and the royal dainties (Genesis 49:20), and those who are His brethren find fruitfulness in service, fellowship with the saints, have a constant resource in the Holy Spirit, walk superior to every adverse condition, and grow stronger with increasing days. Very special will be the joy of Him Who has loved us in displaying the result of His love, the manifested outshining of Divine affection which the flashing lustre of the onyx symbolizes. In His own words, "That the world may know that Thou lovest them as Thou hast loved Me" (John 17:23).

12. *Jasper* ({*'yashapheh'*}}. The Septuagint reads (*ὀνύχιον*) instead of jasper. This is better perhaps 'Diamond' and is the last stone in the breastplate. This stone with the Sardius (ruby) is associated in the Sitter on the throne in Revelation 4. Its symbolism is given in Revelation 21:11 as representative of the glory of God, and with this is connected the joy of Revelation 20:6 and the happiness of Him Who cometh in the Name of the Lord (Psalm 118:26). In this last Scripture, the word *'barak'* = 'praise' is substituted for *'asher'* as more indicative of a festivity of praise and holy joy in which the whole assembly of the unseen world will participate. On this stone was inscribed the name of Naphtali = 'my wrestling'; for the glorious day of God's glory and victory will celebrate the result of the wrestling of the heart of God with sin and death which threatened His creation with catastrophic ruin. He gave His Son in love

supreme to enter the lists against the foe whose final overthrow shall issue in the triumphant acclaim of Revelation 19:6-7. How beautifully does this lead on to the thought enshrined in the Jasper (Diamond) so characteristic of the Holy City, New Jerusalem. It is there said to be clear as crystal (Revelation 21:11), and from this we may gather that the diamond is the stone intended[46]; and this perhaps for another reason: the diamond is crystalised carbon, and what greater contrast could there be than between the blackness of this substance and the brilliance of the gem. How representative is this of the transforming grace that has wrought by redemption upon material so unsuitable as sinful man, and produced by the power of Divine love that which shall transmit unhindered in its brightest display the excellence of every attribute of God. Yes, God has made His own Son to be sin for us, Who knew no sin, that we might become the righteousness of God in Him.

The glory of God in its brightest display, as far as it can be seen and imparted to the creature, shall be displayed in dazzling radiance made more intense by the unsullied light which falls upon and shines through it. For the diamond, the most indestructible of jewels, and the nearest to the pure ray of light in its lustre, has no light in itself, but possesses the quality of transmitting the excellence of the least ray of light that falls upon it. It is perhaps well to remind ourselves that there is that in the glory of the Supreme Being of God which is far beyond creature power to know, for in the dignity of His own proper Godhead there must always be an infinite distance between God the Creator and the most exalted of His creatures. He dwelleth in light unapproachable

46 The stone now called Jasper is opaque.

Whom no one hath seen nor can see. Nevertheless this glory which cannot be communicated rests in complacent love, and without shade of obscurity or trace of dimness upon that which it has communicated out of its own fulness. Just as the colourless beam of light which falls upon the gem breaks up into its various prismatic rays, so God displays Himself in His all varied wisdom as the Father of lights, exhibiting in Christ and His body which is the Church, the fulness of Him which filleth all in all.

The ruby is the first stone in the breastplate, the diamond (jasper) is the last. Thus in this also the suffering Lamb, and the glory of the Lamb, embracing all the various rays of the stones between, is eloquent.

It is worthy of note that in the Holy City {Revelation 21:19-20} the diamond is the first foundation, for the glory of God is fundamental for stability, and this is why the cities of the nations lacking this must fall. The amethyst, speaking of righteousness reigning, comes last, whilst the two centre stones, 6th and 7th, are ruby and chrysolite = death and resurrection[47]. The Church has her origin in glory, and this is where Paul's gospel begins, with a glorified Christ. The Cross is central, for apart from this, the great end of sharing Christ's glory and reigning with Him could never have become actual.

All this is now secured in the Holiest of all, answering to the jewelled breastplate upon the heart of Christ. He is the anointed Priest, constituted as such after the order of Melchisedek by the finality of the oath of God (Psalm 110). Gracious and tender is He indeed seeking to lift us, in the sympathy of His heart on which our names are written, above our infirmities and sorrows, and to lead

47 The witness of righteousness and judgment (Acts 17:31).

us in company with Himself to worship the Father in Spirit and in Truth, Urim and Thummim. For this He has declared unto us that Name ineffable in order that the love wherewith He is loved may be in us, and He in us to give His own character of Son to the response of worship which He leads.

We cannot do better than close our meditation on the breastplate with the words of C. H. Macintosh:

> "The peculiar excellence of a precious stone is seen in this, that the more intense the light which is brought to bear upon it, the more brightly it shines. Light can never make a precious stone look dim, it only increases and develops its lustre. The 12 tribes were each maintained in the Divine Presence in all that undimmed lustre and unalterable beauty which belonged to the position in which the perfect grace of the God of Israel had set them. Whatever might be their infirmities, their errors or their failures, yet their names glittered on the breastplate with unfailing brilliance. Who could penetrate into the Holy Place to snatch from Aaron's breast the name of one of Israel's tribes? Not one. They lay beyond the reach of every enemy, beyond the influence of every evil. We may have to confess and mourn over our constant failures and shortcomings; the eye may, at times, be so dimmed with the tears of genuine contrition as to be but little able to catch the lustre of the precious stones on which our names are engraven, yet there they are all the while. God sees them and that is enough. He is glorified by

> their brightness — a brightness not of our attaining but of His imparting."[48]

It was our Lord Himself Who said, "In this rejoice not, that the spirits are subject unto you; but rather rejoice, because your names are written in heaven" (Luke 10:20)[49].

### SUMMARY: THE TWELVE JEWELS

The following may help the memory.

| | | |
|---|---|---|
| | ( 1. Ruby (sardius) | Redemption |
| Death | ( 2. Topaz | Recompense |
| | ( 3. Carbuncle | Satisfaction |
| | ( 4. Emerald | Sonship |
| Resurrection | ( 5. Sapphire | Declaration |
| | ( 6. Sardonyx (diamond) | Gathering |
| | ( 7. Ligure (jacinth) | Fruitfulness |
| Ascension | ( 8. Agate | Forgetfulness |
| | ( 9. Amethyst | Supremacy |
| | (10. Beryl (chrysolite) | Administration |
| Manifestation | (11. Onyx | Jubilation |
| | (12. Diamond (jasper) | Victory |

"They shall be Mine saith the Lord of Hosts in that day … My jewels" (Malachi 3:17).

48 C. H. Macintosh, *Notes on Exodus*, page 296

49 Graven upon the onyx stones {Exodus 28:9, 39:6}; the breastplate {Exodus 28:21, 39:14}; the palms of My hands (Isaiah 49:16).

### Summary: The Twelve Tribes

| | |
|---|---|
| 1. Judah | = praise (Genesis 29:35) |
| 2. Issachar | = hire or recompense |
| 3. Zebulon | = dwelling |
| 4. Reuben | = see a son |
| 5. Simeon | = hearing (Levi = joined) |
| 6. Gad | = a troop or company |
| 7. Ephraim | = fruitful (Genesis 41:52) |
| 8. Manasseh | = forgetting (Genesis 41:51) |
| 9. Benjamin | = son of the right hand (Genesis 35:18) (Benoni = son of my sorrow) |
| 10. Dan | = judging {Genesis 49:16} (Dinah= judgment; Daniel = God is my Judge) |
| 11. Asher | = happy or blessed |
| 12. Naphtali | = my wrestling {Genesis 30:8} (wrestlings of God; compare Genesis 32:24{-30}) |

## The Holy Plate

This was a plate of pure gold fastened by a lace of blue upon the forefront of the mitre, and upon it the words were engraved *'Kodesh l' Jehovah'*, = 'Holiness to the Lord'. Aaron was to wear this upon his forehead always when exercising his priestly office, in order that the iniquity of the holy things, in the holy gifts which the children of Israel consecrated to the Lord, should not hinder their acceptance before Him.

At first sight we are startled by the mutual repellence indicated by the putting together of such words as Holy and Iniquity, and this too in connection, not with man in his unregenerate state, but with those recognised as the people of God, and whose gifts were offered according to the ordinance of God. The first thought conveyed is that of the white searchlight of God's holiness, which is far beyond the best estimation of the holiest of men. The next is the sense of imperfection and defilement on our part as worshippers, and our inability to present any act of worship or service wholly suitable to the Divine Presence.

Lastly, these two considerations should produce in us deep thankfulness for the provision of such a Priest through Whose acceptance in Divine righteousness our feeble earth-stained worship and service is presented in accordance with the holiness of the eternal throne. Thus, as we have so great a Priest over the House of God and One Whose personal acceptance cannot be brought in question, we have liberty to draw near, knowing that the same brow, once so thorn-scarred, is radiant with the suitability of all His redeemed in Him, to dwell in the light unstained of the holiness of God. It is by Him we can offer sacrifices of praise to God continually, that is the fruit of our lips, giving thanks to His Name. How acceptable surely is the feeblest believer in the Name of the Beloved of God. Not in righteousness of law, for no golden plate bears that writing in the Holiest of God, but in righteousness which is of God by faith through Christ.

Three articles of priestly attire were engraved like the engravings of a signet, the names on the shoulder stones, the names on the breastplate, and the inscription on the Holy Plate. In each case there was no possibility of erasure, and as a signet is that with which an impression is made, so a result answering thereto should be produced upon those upon whom the high honour is bestowed of being represented in the heavenly sanctuary. The onyx on the shoulder speaks of *strength*, therefore I should be always confident because I have His strength. The breastplate on the heart speaks of *love*, therefore I should be always rejoicing because I have His love. The golden plate speaks of *acceptance*; therefore I should be always a worshipper in the consciousness of having received Sonship in the Beloved, Who is *a Holy Priest*.

When the Melchisedek Priesthood of our Lord Jesus Christ shall irradiate this earth, and make the place of His feet glorious, then shall rise glad response from rejoicing hearts to the bright world above, and upon the bells of the horses, and upon every pot in Judah and Jerusalem shall be "Holiness to the Lord". The traffic of the city and the domesticity of the home shall be vocal with the praise of the beauty of holiness (Zechariah 14:20-21; compare 1 Chronicles 16:28-31, Psalm 29:2, Psalm 96:9).

Is it not a privilege to antedate that coming day, and ere we leave the matters of our earthly sojourn and join the countless multitude on high, to yield all our concerns into the hands of our Great High Priest, that from business and family circle He may eliminate everything upon which He cannot write, "Holiness to the Lord".

The *lace of blue* shows the connection of Divine love with holiness, and this binding the plate upon the mitre indicates that the exercise of our Lord's priestly grace will never fail until the objects of His care belonging to the priestly family both Holy and Royal, and whether heavenly or earthly in calling, shall reach the place assigned to them in the Divine purpose.

### The Mitre

The word mitre (*mits-neh-feth*) comes from the Latin and Greek *'mitra'*, a fillet or turban; the Hebrew word signifies a diadem. Originally the diadem indicated the blue and white band worn by Asiatic monarchs around the royal headdress.

The golden plate sets forth our Lord as a Holy Priest, whilst this last article of priestly attire, the mitre, designates His glory as *a Royal {or reigning} Priest*, and to Him the diadem belongs by double right.

The crowning day is coming, for there is a glory not yet fulfilled, a glory having its own special character, a glory belonging to Christ which the type of Melchisedek teaches us. When the display of this is revealed then the title of the Most High God, Possessor of heaven and earth, shall be established in Him in Whom all things shall be gathered in one. What rich blessing shall ensue when the Most High God makes good His title of Possessor of heaven and earth in His High Priest,

Whom His grace has given us now to know as ours before He is revealed to the astonishment of the nations (Isaiah 52:15). All other gods will then be excluded, Jehovah shall be One and His Name One. Under His righteous sway the very ends of the earth shall feel the blessing of His pervading, comprehensive blessedness.

Melchisedek was by interpretation King of righteousness and King of peace (Hebrews 7{:1-2}), and our Lord's Melchisedek priesthood shall be the security of peace, the fruit of righteousness, and in effect quietness and assurance for ever. The Melchisedek priesthood is characterized by blessing and intercession with which our Lord and Priest is at present exercised after the pattern of His High Priestly prayer of John 17. We know His Priesthood is after the order of Melchisedek, secured by oath in perpetuity, and we rejoice as happy worshippers within the vail, before the God and Father of our Lord Jesus Christ. Meanwhile Israel is waiting for the blessing of Numbers 6:24-27 until they shall see Him as Priest come forth, the witness to them of the acceptance of the blood of atonement carried within the vail.

The mitre of fine linen carries our thoughts back to the same material used in the curtains of the court. In both cases it is representative of the character of Christ and it is this, and not the character of Adam, that shall bring peace and rest to this troubled world, when He shall reign as Priest upon His throne.

In conclusion, may the blessing of the priestly service of our Lord on high refresh our spirits; may our ears be attuned to catch the sweet melodies of heaven, the praises He leads, until, called to be with Him in the Father's House, it will be our joy to see Him glorified in the place of His suffering and to hear Him acclaimed, by a creation delivered from the bondage of corruption, as King of Kings and Lord of Lords.

### Resumé of the Priestly Garments

A resumé of the priestly garments is as follows:–

1. The embroidered linen coat representing a *gracious* priest.
2. The inner girdle representing a *serving* priest.
3. The blue robe of the ephod representing a *loving* priest.
4. The ephod representing a *great* priest.
5. The curious girdle of the ephod representing a *worshipping* priest.
6. The onyx stones representing a *mighty* priest.
7. The breastplate representing a *representative* priest.
8. The holy plate representing a *holy* priest.
9. The mitre representing a *reigning* priest.

When the Father's house resoundeth
  With the music and the song:
When the bride in glorious raiment
  Sees the One Who loved so long;
Then for new and blessed service
  Girt afresh will He appear,
Stand and serve before His angels
  Those who waited for Him here.
He will bring them where the fountains
  Fresh and full spring forth above,
Still throughout the endless ages
  Serving in the joy of love.[50]

T.P.

50 {(T.P.) Mrs Emma Frances Bevan (1827-1909), written at home at Trent Park, East Barnet}

# Chapter 20: The Divine Presence

A few words may be added in respect of the symbol of the Divine Presence that accompanied the children of Israel from Egypt to the land of God's purpose for them.

Its first appearance was at Etham in the wilderness that bordered on the Egypt side of the Red Sea. Just when all that spoke of civilisation and resource was at an end, when the cities of Rameses and the villages of Succoth were left behind and a trackless waste lay ahead, this was when they proved that "Man's extremity is God's opportunity"[51].

The cloud was the symbol of the Divine Presence, it was their guide, their shelter, their defence, the pledge that God would bring them into the mountain of His inheritance. Psalm 105:39 says, "He spread a cloud for a covering", and how grateful such a protection must have been from the overpowering heat of the fierce rays of the sun in a cloudless sky. The cloud was the constant evidence of the minute care of God for His people. He was concerned in all their doings, nothing was too great or too little in their lives for His personal interest in

51 {John Flavell (1627-1691)}

them, and we too may learn from this that no less is His care for His saints today, "Casting all your care upon Him, for *He careth for you.*"

The Divine Presence was in the cloud. Doubtless it was the same cloud that enveloped the astonished disciples on the Holy Mount; the same which received the Lord Jesus when He ascended from Olivet; the same in which He will return when His feet shall again touch the earth at that sacred spot. The movements of the cloud must often have tested the faith and patience of Moses and the people. Taken up, as the word of command to march, sometimes by day, sometimes by night. Lingering so long in one place, as if it had forgotten to move, or again ceaselessly moving as though it would never stop. Yet never mistaking the way, they were led on by His powerful, omnipotent hand. Their one attitude was to be dependent, their one business to follow day by day. To wait thus on the God Whom we have known, to spend our days with Him, is the present path of peace, where rest, true rest, is found.

These patterns of the things in the heavens, a shadow of good things to come, have their present answer in the realised presence of God with His own who wait for that day. It is to be hoped that our study of these types may leave an impress on our hearts of the exceeding blessedness belonging to that presence, and to a more diligent appreciation of the glorious worth of Him, Who, having removed every barrier by the sacrifice of Himself, gives, not as the world, but shares all He possesses with His loved co-heirs.

His presence there, my soul
Its rest, its joy untold
Shall find, when endless ages roll,
And time shall ne'er grow old.[52]

Now by His Spirit He abides, the earnest of the end when God shall be all in all. The millennial day shall witness the cloud of glory once again as the glowing prophecy of Isaiah relates (chapter 4:5).

"Then Jehovah creates on the dwellings of Zion,
And on all her assemblies, a cloud and a smoke;
These shall provide a shade in the daytime
That turns to a fire bright shining by night;
For high over all shall hover the glory."[53]

Then in the blest state eternal, the Lamb of God with His Church prepared as a bride adorned for her husband, shall be the tabernacle in which God will dwell with men, they His people and God Himself their God. Tears, death, sorrow, crying, gone, with every trace of sin that caused the pain to God and His creation. Then through the universe shall reverberate like a single stroke upon the bell of Eternity, the words of Him that sits upon the throne (Revelation 21:6),

"IT IS DONE".

J.G. 10.3.36.

52 {John Nelson Darby (1800-1882)}

53 {Frederick Charles Jennings (1847-1948), *Studies in Isaiah*, Loizeaux Brothers, 1935, page 45}

# Appendix 1: The History of the Ark[54]

Every reader of the Old Testament must be impressed with the place which the Ark of the Covenant fills in the inspired record. As far as time is concerned its history covers a space of over one thousand years. Constructed by Divine direction in the first year of the wilderness journey from Egypt to Canaan, and accompanying the hosts of Israel during their forty years' wanderings, it became the centre of attention at the crossing of the Jordan and the taking of Jericho. After this the ark remained at Gilgal for seven years until the division of the land was completed, when it was transferred to the tabernacle set up in Shiloh. During the troublous times of the judges it remained in this place for about four hundred and thirty years, until the death of Eli, when it was captured by the Philistines at the battle of Aphek. This point is a crisis in its history. Hitherto the glory of God had rested upon the mercy seat, now this was so no longer; Ichabod, the glory is departed, was written upon Israel. Psalm 78:56-64 shows what led up to this and the serious change that had taken place. Up to this time the

54 James Green, *Scripture Truth*, volume 7 (1915), pages 298-300.

ark is looked at in connection with the inheritance and the promises and purposes of God. Jordan is the death and resurrection of Christ; Jericho, the victorious power belonging to His place in the heavenlies; Gilgal is the sentence of death upon the flesh; and Shiloh the peace that follows. The deliverance of His strength into captivity, and His glory into the enemy's hand, sets forth the death of Christ from another point of view, namely, the heir, David, and the sure mercies connected with him.

To return to the history, after being seven months with the Philistines, the ark was restored to Israel, and a place was found for it in the house of Abinadab at Kirjath-jearim. Here it remained undisturbed for twenty years until the battle of Mizpeh. In the seventy years that follow, during the judgeship of Samuel, the reign of Saul and the first ten years of David's reign, little is heard of the ark. It would seem to have been carried about to various places, for it was with the army at Gibeah (1 Samuel 14:18), and probably was also at Nob under the care of Ahimelech. However, after the destruction of that city by Doeg the Edomite (1 Samuel 22:19), we find it again in the house of Abinadab. From this place David sought to remove it, and when his ill-advised attempt had ended in disaster, Obededom the Gittite became its custodian for three months. Great was the rejoicing, when in the appointed manner the ark was brought to Zion and placed in the tent that David had prepared for it; this was its abode for forty-one years. The place which it had in the affections of David is touchingly set forth in Psalm 132:1-8. During the remainder of his days the king ever resorted to it as the symbol of God's presence with His people, and his faith ever recognised that the ark was the pledge of God's covenant, although no Shekinah glory had dwelt upon it from the days of Shiloh. And faith also now is fully assured that although as yet no manifested glory has crowned the blessed person of our Lord Jesus Christ, nevertheless, He is the pledge of the fulfilment of every promise of God, in the coming days of His Solomon reign. Meanwhile how precious is it to seek Him in the secret place and learn the depths of Divine love and counsel which centre in Him; and, like David, to rejoice in the grace which takes account of those who in themselves are unworthy after the order of the man of high degree.

Then in the history of Israel came the day when the temple of Solomon was completed, and the ark was placed in the Holy of Holies, the staves by which it had been long carried were removed and the glory of God once more rested upon it. Patiently for four hundred and twenty years God was in the midst of His people, bearing with their sin and folly until there was no remedy. The hosts of the Chaldeans were allowed to lay siege to doomed Jerusalem, and then slowly and sorrowfully the glory left its place between the cherubims and the long sentence of "not my people" was written upon the nation. From this time all mention of the ark ceases, it probably perished in the destruction of the vessels by Nebuchadnezzar (2 Kings 24:13). Jewish tradition says that it was preserved by Jeremiah, but there is no evidence to support this, and Jeremiah 3:16 is against it. The Holiest of the second temple was empty, and when Christ, the true Ark of the Covenant, came to His own, His own received Him not, nor shall the excellent glory be manifest in the midst of the nation, until they shall say, "blessed is He that cometh in the name of the Lord."

We may gather from what has been said that the history of the ark is divided into four parts: (1) in the wilderness; (2) in the land; (3) in its time of obscurity; (4) in the glory of the kingdom. Christ is the Antitype of the ark in these four ways. Firstly, He was here on earth in wilderness circumstances; He tabernacled amongst men, He was the revelation of God and His oracle, for God was speaking in His Son. In His heart the law was hidden, and in His life it was fulfilled. But, secondly, the land, the purpose of God was before Him, and passing the Jordan of His death and resurrection, He has entered into possession of the inheritance, the true Canaan, the heavenly places. Thirdly, still here on earth it is the time of His rejection and obscurity. Men will seek His help in times of stress, and pray to Him to further their schemes of national advancement; but there is no place in this vast world system for Him, nor can there be except in those hearts which grace has opened, and in those homes where affection for Him reigns, and who make Him a place as did Abinadab, Obededom, and David.

Presently the remnant of Israel will seek to find Him a house of rest, and turning to the stone which the builders have rejected, they will refuse to give sleep to their eyes or slumber to their eyelids, until they find out a place for Jehovah, a habitation for the mighty God of Jacob. Like John in Revelation 11:19, they will look up to see their Messiah, the true Ark of the Covenant, in heaven, the security, the Yea and the Amen of all the promises of God to their nation. Then, fourthly, when He shall have unrolled, with its accompanying judgments, the scroll of the inheritance of the earth, that glorious kingdom shall come, and He shall sit upon the throne of His glory; the house more magnificent, the kingdom more blessed, the glory more excellent than its foreshadowing in the days of Solomon. The true place of the ark on Zion shall be seen in Christ, Jehovah's choice, His dwelling-place and His rest for ever; and Christ shall be acknowledged as the true Shekinah, the effulgence of the glory of God.

Returning again to the history something further may be gathered. The last mention of the ark is in the days of Josiah (2 Chronicles 35:3). But although the desire of the good king was to turn the hearts of the people once more to God, and recall them to God's centre, their regard for the ark had that superstitious character with which they looked upon the idols they reverenced. So the ark, like the serpent of brass in the days of Hezekiah, must disappear, and Jeremiah's word to them was that they should no longer have it as an object before them. In the days to come when Israel shall be restored to their land, they shall not say, "The Ark of the Covenant of the Lord; neither shall it come to mind; neither shall they remember it; neither shall they visit it; neither shall it be magnified ({Authorized version} margin) any more" (Jeremiah 3:16-17). The name of the Lord shall take the place of the ark as God's gathering centre for all nations. So when the Holy Spirit mentions the ark in Hebrews 9:1-5, with other vessels of the sanctuary, He says, we cannot now speak of these particularly or in detail; they are types which have passed now that the reality has come in Christ. It is noticeable that in this passage no mention is made of the altars of incense and burnt-offering, and on comparing Ezekiel 41:22 and 43:13-17, we find that these two vessels and these only have a place in that glorious millennial temple of victory and praise. This is exceedingly beautiful, for the sacrifices which will be offered on the one, and the incense on the other, will be the continual remembrance of the victorious work of Calvary and the praise and worship which will arise in the fragrance of Christ. No ark will be needed, for He will be there in person; no shewbread for a memorial, for all Israel will be gathered; no candlestick, for the Spirit will be poured out upon all flesh; no laver, for a fountain will be opened to the house of David for sin and for uncleanness.

# Appendix 2: Invitation to a series of Addresses by the Author in Manchester in the 1930s

EVERY SATURDAY EVENING
at 7-30.
ADDRESSES TO BELIEVERS.

EVERY SUNDAY EVENING
at 6-30.
GOSPEL ADDRESS.

*ALL ARE WELCOME.*

CROMWELL HALL,
CROMWELL GROVE, LEVENSHULME.

SIX ADDRESSES

will be given (D.V.) on

*The Tabernacle in the Wilderness.*

By Mr. JAMES GREEN (London).

LARGE OIL PAINTINGS BY THE LECTURER
will be used to illustrate the Series.

*Syllabus of Meetings.*

**Saturday, February 15th, at 7-30 p.m.**

1. The Court of the Tabernacle ... ... ... ... ... ... *The way of approach through Christ*

**Sunday, February 16th, at 6-30 p.m.**

2. The Altar and the Laver ... ... ... ... ... ... ... ... ... *The atoning work of Christ*

**Tuesday, February 18th, at 8 p.m.**

3. The Tabernacle and its Coverings ... ... ... ... ... ... *The varied glories of Christ*

**Thursday, February 20th, at 8 p.m.**

4. The Vessels of the Holy Place ... ... ... ... ... ... *The Light and Food found in Christ*

**Saturday, February 22nd, at 7-30 p.m.**

5. The Ark and the Holiest of all ... ... ... ... ... ... *The Deity and Humanity of Christ*

**Sunday, February 23rd, at 6-30 p.m.**

6. The Robes of the High Priest ... ... ... ... ... ... ... ... ... *The Priesthood of Christ*

You are heartily invited to come to these Addresses.

PLEASE BRING YOUR OWN BIBLES. NO COLLECTIONS.

CPSIA information can be obtained
at www.ICGtesting.com
Printed in the USA
BVHW062216280321
603623BV00004B/564

9 780951 151563